D1588335

In the Saddle

In the Saddle

In the Saddle
Exploits of the 5th Georgia Cavalry

Timothy Daiss

Schiffer Military History
Atglen, PA

DEDICATION

In Memory of:
My mother
Shirley Barnard Daiss (1936-1991)

My grandfather
George Barnard (1911-1975)

And his grandfather
Jonathan D. Barnard (1844-1930)
5th Georgia Cavalry
Company H
Confederate States Army

Book Design by Ian Robertson.
Copyright © 1999 by Timothy Daiss.
Library of Congress Catalog Number: 99-63328

Printed in China.
ISBN: 0-7643-0972-2

We are interested in hearing from authors with book ideas on related topics.

Published by Schiffer Publishing Ltd.
4880 Lower Valley Road
Atglen, PA 19310
Phone: (610) 593-1777
FAX: (610) 593-2002
E-mail: Schifferbk@aol.com.
Visit our web site at: www.schifferbooks.com
Please write for a free catalog.
This book may be purchased from the publisher.
Please include $3.95 postage.
Try your bookstore first.

In Europe, Schiffer books are distributed by:
Bushwood Books
6 Marksbury Road
Kew Gardens
Surrey TW9 4JF
England
Phone: 44 (0)181 392-8585
FAX: 44 (0)181 392-9876
E-mail: Bushwd@aol.com.

Try your bookstore first.

Contents

INTRODUCTION

When I began this project it was an effort to learn more about my great-great grandfather's Civil War regiment. Soon, I became engrossed in the pursuit. From my first readings of the 5th Georgia Cavalry in the *Official Records of the War of the Rebellion* to the last word of this work, I have been both fascinated and enthralled by the bravery, sacrifice, and suffering of the men in this unit. Their exploits have permeated my imagination, and more than once I have awakened in the night with the sound of gun fire and the thunder of horse hooves echoing in my mind.

Yet, the men and women of this generation suffered tremendous adversity and heartache, and no amount of imagination can come close to experiencing what they endured. From the families who sent sons off to war who never returned, to the boys who fought in the ranks, theirs was a unique experience, a unique generation.

It is in this light that I offer this present work. It is told by the soldiers themselves, with the exception of reminiscences of the war by a veteran's wife. It is their voice reaching out to us from the past, "stop, look, listen and I'll tell you a tale."

In preparing the manuscript a decision was made to use only a portion of the letters, narratives, and memoirs that were found. In this capacity, it serves more as a primer than a regimental history. It offers the best selection of writings by the men in the 5th Georgia rather than a long and exhausting account of the unit's every movement. Hopefully, it captures the general sentiment and emotion of those days so long ago.

Though this work tells the story of a southern military unit, brave men and boys, North and South, gave their life's blood for their convictions. To them we must pay homage and perpetuate their memory.

Tim Daiss

1

In Search of Johnny Reb

I was born with a RebelYell in my throat and Dixie on my tongue.
Rebel blood courses through my veins.

Some of my earliest memories go back to my childhood conversations that I had with my mother. She was a patriot, an American patriot, but also a southern patriot. She instilled in me a thirst for knowledge, a love of reading, writing, and history, but also *the pride of being a Southerner.*

My mother was born in the 1930s, the first of three children. When she was a child there were a few men still alive who had worn gray, though they were considerably old. In fact, she would tell the story of how, as a small child, she would play on the floor next to an elderly great uncle who had a wooden leg with holes carved through it. She would run her small fingers through these holes, surely to the delight and amusement of her uncle. She recalled with pride that this uncle had lost his leg in the *The War for Southern Independence.*

As my mother grew up she experienced what it was like to be a southerner and visit other parts of the country, to experience first hand the negative stereotypes that prevailed against the South and her people. She recalled a high-school trip to New York during the 1950s. Her bus was in a parking lot next to a school bus of New York students. She vividly recalled what transpired: The New Yorkers scoffed at the southerners. They mimicked their accents and shouted obscenities. This experience would stay with her for the rest of her life, thus confirming the opinion of many that the South was a country within a country, a conquered nation, an occupied people, who were regarded by their fellow countrymen as second class citizens. I have also experienced this on occasion, though, for the most part, it is passing away.

Another early memory in my life was my family's trip to *Six Flags over Georgia* in Atlanta in 1970. My older brothers wanted souvenirs, so my father bought them blue Civil War caps, *kepis*, but this didn't set well with my mother! She bought a Confederate gray kepi and proudly placed it on my head. It is here that my heritage began to take root, though at the time I didn't know it, nor could I have comprehended it.

I also recall playing in my back yard with blue and gray plastic Civil War soldiers. I would align the opposing armies for battle. With rocks and marbles, the artillery shells would burst, men would fall, and troops would fall back and regroup. The sound of musketry filled the air, horses galloped, and flags fluttered in the breeze. Of course, the men in gray always took the day, while the Federals skedaddled in the face of a fierce Rebel Yell. In fact, as a small boy, I would innocently remark that the only war America had ever lost was the Civil War and Custer's Last Stand. I thought that everyone had southern sympathies and that it was the accepted way of thought. I'm not quite sure how I became acquainted with the flamboyant, long-haired Michigan cavalryman, but soon learned that he had not worn gray during the war.

By my teen-age years my awe of the war took a back seat to more pressing issues—cars and girls. But, by this age, I was already a Rebel patriot.

> *Your bare feet and tattered clothes haunt me,*
> *I hear a musket, minnie balls fill the air,*
> *"Double quick, volley, give 'em the cold steel boys!"*
> *Battle flags torn and bloody,*
> *Comrades slain and wounded,*
> *Tossing and turning I try to wake,*
> *But fall again into slumber,*
> *I see you at a distance,*
> *an image sketched in my mind,*
> *as a sentinel on guard walking through the years with me,*

*I awaken now, but quickly close my eyes and
the image is still there.*

Through my college years I retained a reverence for history, particularly Civil War history. Ironically, I seldom read about the war, other than brief summaries and outlines of battles and events. The war seemed to contain a sense of sorrow and loss, a bitter sweetness—perhaps the enigma of the Lost Cause. Not that I defend slavery, I abhor it. But the men and boys who fought in the ranks seldom owned slaves, nor fought for the institution. They reacted to an increasingly overbearing Federal government and did what most men would do when backed into a corner and hearth, home, and family are threatened—they fought, and did so valiantly for four full years. They fought until their homes were burnt and their hearts melted away.

In late 1991, I finished graduate school and returned to Savannah. In less than two months I would experience the untimely death of my mother. This marked a crossroads in my life. She was the glue that held the family together; things would never be the same. The next 12 months were a blur.

The year is 1993. The Georgia General Assembly is in session. Governor Zell Miller proposes the removal of the Confederate emblem form the state flag. A political war erupts. It is here that I am reminded of my heritage. When I first heard the news, I accepted it. "After all, this was the last decade of the twentieth century. I'm open minded and not stuck in the traditions of the past. Anyway, who wants to defend something so politically incorrect?" I said to a friend one day at lunch. While I rationalized with all of the arguments, something deep within churned. "No! They can't change the flag," I heard myself say aloud one morning while pouring over news coverage of the assembly. The Confederate within emerged. Why was I having such a response? A quick look back and the answer was obvious. What had been dormant for years now emerged with vigor and strength. Letters were dispatched to editors of various newspapers, calls were made, and I took a stand. I began to devour books on the war, not just summaries or brief outlines, but biographies, letters, diaries, first hand battle accounts, and anything I could get my hands on. In less than a year, I became well acquainted with every major battle of the war and many not-so-famous ones.

But, what about my ancestors? What part did they play? Aching to find out, I began an odyssey of the heart and soul. I looked for names, specific names of family members who had served during the war, but could not find any. "How could this be?" If my mother were still alive, she could surely tell me, but I was on my own. What transpired was a year long search that should have taken only a few months. I began a genealogical search on my mother's maiden name, Barnard.

My father's family was from the Midwest and had, as recently as the late nineteenth century, immigrated from Ireland and Germany.

I traced the Barnards back to the eighteenth century. James Barnard, my great-great-great-great grandfather, settled in south Georgia in 1820; he was from Massachusetts. His father, John Barnard (1753-1813) of Boston, a descendant of Roger Williams (1603-1683), the banished Baptist clergyman and founder of Rhode Island, had fought the British as a soldier in the Continental Army. I now had names of seven generations of Barnards. Two were of military age during the Civil War, Daniel Barnard (born 1818) and Jonathan D. Barnard (born 1844). I searched in vain for a listing in the *Roster of Confederate Soldiers from Georgia*. This work (which has been updated to include all Confederate military personnel) listed only veterans who served in the infantry. It never occurred to me that my family members may have served the Confederacy in another capacity. After a few contacts with the Georgia Department of Archives and History, I discovered that Daniel Barnard's name appeared on the *Militia Enrollment List Compiled as Required by the State of Georgia, for the 401st District of Tattnall County, Georgia.* Further research indicated that he did not see active service during the war. But what about Jonathan D. Barnard? A few weeks later my persistence paid off.

I discovered that Jonathan D. Barnard enlisted in the 2nd Georgia Cavalry Battalion at the age of 19 on July 11, 1862. In a few months this battalion became part of the newly organized 5th Georgia Volunteer Cavalry. He fought against Sherman's troops as they pressed against Atlanta. Just before Atlanta fell, his brigade moved into Tennessee.

Jonathan was wounded in a skirmish in Tennessee in late October 1864 and was sent to south Georgia for 60 days on a wounded furlough. While recovering from his wounds, he became ill with what the doctors called the "fever." He recovered in March, 1865 and tried to make his way back to his unit, but by now Sherman had completed his march through Georgia and all the roads and bridges were guarded. Jonathan was captured by Yankee pickets, but escaped the same night. A few weeks passed and the war came to a close.

In 1911 Jonathan D. Barnard applied for, and received, a Confederate pension from the state of Georgia. He died at the grand old age of 86, and is buried beneath a military head stone in the Antioch Baptist Church cemetery in Evans County, Georgia.

On my first trip to the Barnard plot to visit Jonathan, I was in for a surprise. I could now recall having visited here over 20 years ago with my mother, brothers, grandfather, numerous aunts, uncles, and cousins. My young memory had betrayed me.

The results of my research were fulfilling beyond expression. I felt that I had found a missing part of myself. Indeed, I was a Georgian, for my family had moved here—nigh two centuries ago. Indeed, I was a *Confederate*.

What made this discovery even richer was the longevity of Jonathan D. Barnard's life (1844-1930). His life crossed paths with my grandfather, George Barnard (1911-1975). My grandfather was a major influence during the first part of my life. He was the only positive, adult, male role model that I had as a boy. I recall spending endless star-filled summer nights with him on his porch, as he would rock in his chair, spin yarns, and chew tobacco. Much of the content of the conversations have receded into the back of my mind as the years have unfolded. But I am still in awe. My own dear grandfather was the grandson of a Johnny Reb. I can picture him seated at the foot of Jonathan, his grandfather, soaking up every word to pass them on to my mother and to me. History has a way of reaching its hand across the generations.

It is now clear. The questions have been answered and the circle is complete. I have found my Johnny Reb.

The guns of Atlanta, Shiloh, and Manassas
course through my mind,
I hear the sound of musket and the clash of sabre,
I see tears, I smell blood, I see death, I see glory,
I taste the battlefield.
Was not I born for such a time as this?
Was not I conceived for such an hour?
I am exalted,
I smite my breast,
I am a Confederate!

2

History of the 5th Georgia Volunteer Cavalry

As the storm clouds of war approached, the South prepared for war. Local militia groups, active in the South before the war, grew busy, and young men filled their ranks. Others formed new military units. In coastal Georgia, two cavalry battalions were formed from such units. The 1st Georgia Cavalry Battalion was formed during the summer of 1862 and consisted of two companies. Their history is difficult to trace, and it is probable that the 1st Georgia Cavalry Battalion didn't participate in any engagements. The 2nd Georgia Cavalry Battalion was also formed in the summer of 1862 and was commanded by Lieutenant Colonel Edward Bird. They engaged Federal troops in light skirmishing on a number of occasions.

Both battalions served on the coast, guarding the numerous rivers, inlets, and water ways of south Georgia and the lower part of South Carolina. The two battalions were consolidated on January 20, 1863, and became the 5th Georgia Cavalry. The new regiment consisted of ten companies, all from coastal Georgia.

Company A - The Georgia Hussars
Company B - The Chatham Light Horse Troop
Company C - The Blue Cap Troop
Company D - The Liberty Guards
Company E - The Bullock Troop
Company F - The Screven Troop

Company G - The Liberty Independent Troop

Company H - The Lamar Mounted Rifles, also known as Lamar Rangers, mostly from Tattnall County

Company I - The Effingham Troop

Company K - The McIntosh Troop

Robert H. Anderson was appointed colonel of the new regiment. Anderson, a native Savannahian and 1857 graduate of the United States Military Academy, had recently served as lieutenant of infantry at Fort Columbus, New York (1857-58), and on frontier duty at Fort Walla Walla, Washington (1858-61). He was on leave when hostilities broke out between North and South, but quickly resigned his commission in the United States Army, returned to Georgia, and was commissioned in the Confederate States Army as lieutenant of artillery on March 16, 1861. In July, 1862 he was appointed major in the 1st Battalion Georgia Sharpshooters. Anderson saw action in February, 1863 (before he assumed command of the 5th Georgia Cavalry) when he successfully held Fort McAlister against bombardment from Union ironclads.

After being formed, the 5th Georgia Cavalry was stationed at Isle of Hope, Georgia, 7 miles south of Savannah. The men of the 5th Georgia were required to furnish their own steeds (a common practice in the Confederate Cavalry) and originally equipped themselves with shot guns; they were issued sabres. Later the troops were issued revolvers and carbines, and also augmented their weaponry from captured Yankee arms.

During this time squads, or detachments of companies from the regiment, would patrol the coast. Occasionally they would skirmish with small numbers of Federal troops, as well as Federal gun boats. Captain O.C. Higgins of Company K describes in a report his frustration with the limited effectiveness of the weapons of the 5th Georgia early in the war: "This company is located in one of the most important and exposed points of the coast, and requires additional forces to protect it. Frequent opportunities occur of destroying the gun boats as they pass up our river, but for want of a cannon they pass without further harm except what they receive from the Maynard rifle and shot gun."

In November, 1863 a detachment of the 5th Georgia Cavalry engaged and repulsed Federal troops at Pocatalligo, South Carolina, and drove them back to their base at Port Royal. The regiment remained in this area for several months and occupied numerous locations, including Adams Run and Green Pond, South Carolina.

In February, 1864 the 5th Georgia Cavalry was dispatched to Florida to help repulse a Federal offensive aimed at restoring the state to the Union. On February 20 fighting broke out at Olustee, about 50 miles south of Jacksonville. Union forces clashed with Confederate forces in fighting that lasted most of the day. By dusk, the Confederates had beaten back the Federals, who retired from the area in a full retreat. The battle of Olustee (Ocean Pond) was the only major military campaign waged in Florida during the war. Detachments of the 5th Georgia Cavalry arrived in time to participate in the battle.

Shortly after the battle of Olustee, the 5th Georgia Cavalry again took up the task of patrolling the coast. At this time Colonel Anderson was becoming impatient with his duties, which he described as, "Unimportant picket duty on the coast." He wanted his regiment to be transferred to active service, preferably in Atlanta.[1]

As Anderson was trying to get his regiment reassigned, the order had already been given for him to join Wheeler's Cavalry Corps, under General Joseph E. Johnston, commander of the Army of Tennessee, to help push back the Federal masses bearing down on Atlanta. Soon, Anderson would have more than he ever bargained for or considered.

The 5th Georgia proceeded to Atlanta via Augusta, where part of the regiment was transported on railroad cars. On June 20, 1864, the 5th Georgia engaged Federals at Noonday Church above Marietta. The battle was indecisive, but the regiment had a taste of things to come. The fighting would be much different than coastal patrol.

The 5th Georgia participated in nearly every major battle of the Atlanta campaign (Noonday Church, Allatoona Hills, Kennesaw Mountain, New Hope Church, Peach Tree Creek, the battle of Atlanta, Jonesboro, Decatur, and Newnan), constantly covering General Johnston's and later General Hood's movements. They also severed enemy communications and raided Union supply lines. They engaged General Edward McCook in his attempt to destroy the last railroad into Atlanta and handed the Federal cavalry a thorough whipping. McCook barely escaped, and the Rebel horseman captured 200 blue clad troopers.

On August 11, 1864, General John Bell Hood, who had recently replaced Johnston as the commander of the Army of Tennessee, ordered Wheeler's cavalry to Tennessee to operate behind enemy lines. Wheeler's route took him to Dalton, where his men destroyed track along the East Tennessee and Georgia Railroad, raided supplies and overwhelmed the Union garrison. From Dalton they passed through Cleveland, Tennessee, cutting and destroying rail road track as they rode. Their raid took them through the heart of Tennessee into Virginia, where they successfully defended government salt works at Gladesville, Virginia, and for a short time hooked forces with the legendary Confederate partisan John Hunt Morgan. After this, Wheeler headed back to Georgia and eventually caught up with Sherman as he was marching toward the sea. Wheeler's troopers were the only force to contend with Sherman on his march. Their objective was to keep the Federal columns in as tight a path as possible, thus minimizing, if possible, their swath of destruction and devastation. As it turned out, Wheeler, only 28 years of age and already a major general, played a game of cat and mouse with his former West Point class mate, Federal cavalry corps commander Judson Kilpatrick. They clashed and skirmished continually.

On December 21, 1864, Sherman's forces occupied Savannah and she was spared the torch. On Christmas eve Sherman wired Abraham Lincoln and presented the city to his commander-in-chief as a Christmas gift. By February, Sherman's troops leisurely crossed into South Carolina. Georgia burned, but South Carolina would be devastated. Sherman's men felt that it was their right to punish the little state that was responsible for starting the "whole damn war."

In South Carolina, the fighting between Confederate and Federal cavalry turned ugly. Wheeler's men found Union stragglers and foragers who had committed atrocities; in response they meted out their own brand of justice. Kilpatrick replied in kind, and a type of guerrilla fighting emerged that most historians make little comment about or mention. After Columbia, South Carolina, fell, Sherman's blue columns moved toward North Carolina. Confederate resistance had all but ceased. The 5th Georgia Cavalry, who had been with Wheeler through all of Georgia and Carolina, was ragged, hungry, and greatly reduced in strength. From a force of 1,000 fighting men they dwindled to a force of less than two hundred. Soon after the battle of Bentonville, North Carolina, Confederate forces surrendered and the men of the 5th Georgia were paroled and sent to Augusta, Georgia. From Augusta they made their way home on foot.

The war was finally over, and lives had to be rebuilt before it made any sense or could be put in perspective. Yet, the men of the 5th Georgia Cavalry had their stories to tell, and as the years passed and the pieces were put back together, they emerged. *In the Saddle: Exploits of the 5th Georgia Cavalry* is their story.

Notes
[1] Charleston and Sav. R.R.
       May 21, 1864
General Braxton Bragg
       Commander in Chief C.S. Army
       Richmond, Virginia

My dear General—

Having once had the honor and pleasure of serving under you at Pensacola Florida as Adjt. General of Gen'l. W.H. Walker's Brigade, I have determined to lay my case before you in a private letter trusting that you will pardon the liberty.

I have been in the Army now General for seven years not including my four at West Point. At the time of the breaking out of the War I was stationed at Fort Walla Walla Washington Territory and resigned my commission the day I received the intelligence of the secession of my state (Georgia) and came immediately home and reported for duty, and was ordered to report to General W.H.T. Walker for duty on his staff in which position I remained until General Walker's resignation, when I was ordered to this department, in which I now have been serving for two years and a half, first on staff duty then as organizer and Commander of the 1st Battalion Sharp Shooters, which command I held until I was promoted to my present Regiment (the 5th Georgia Cavalry) some eighteen months ago. I have made repeated applications to be ordered active service effect. I now appeal to you General as a graduate of West Point, and brother army officer to relieve me from my present false position. I do not ask promotion until I have to your satisfaction won my spurs. I simply beg you to order me into active service with my Regiment to report to General Johnston, for service with Wheeler or to any other active field you may see fit to assign me to. If you cannot spare my Regiment from this Dept. (where it is at present doing nothing but unimportant picket duty on the coast) can you not detach me temporarily as I feel I could render service to Gen. Johnston or Wheeler as an Inspector.

I would as a matter of course prefer going with my Regiment which is in splendid condition, and for months equipment armament drill and discipline I will refer you to Generals Beauregard, W.H.T. Walker, and Patton Anderson who have pronounced it to be the finest regiment of Cavalry they have seen in the Confederate Service, but if I cannot go with my Regiment I would prefer leaving it, to remaining here inactive.

I know General that an officer of your cultivation and eminent military character will appreciate my professional anxiety to get into active service, and will wait patiently, having an abiding faith that you will soon give me an opportunity of drawing my sabre in an active field, for our holy Cause.

If it will be impossible for you to grant my (which I trust to Providence will not be the case) request, please relieve my suspense by writing me a few lines.

With my warmest wishes for your health and success
/signature/ Robert H. Anderson
Endorsement—
"Asking for field service"
"It had been given before recd."
The Georgia Historical Society, Savannah.

3

Three Years of War

The first sketch was written by James T. Lambright of Brunswick, Georgia, in 1910 at the request of the *Clement A. Evans Chapter United Daughters of the Confederacy*. He enlisted in the 5th Georgia Cavalry as a 16 year old boy in 1862 and served for the duration of the war. His narrative covers his regiment's movements from coastal patrol in Georgia, Florida, and South Carolina to fighting around Atlanta, Wheeler's raid in Tennessee and following Sherman through Georgia and the Carolinas.

Though written forty-five years after the end of the war, it should be noted that Lambright conducted careful research before he wrote his narrative and consulted it as he wrote. His facts, as a whole, are supported by primary source documents. One exception to this is his use of numbers when referring to troops and battles. Inaccuracies are cited in the end notes. Lambright's narrative follows:

I was nearly 17 years of age when I enlisted in May, 1862. The Troop was then encamped at Palmyra, near Sunbury, Liberty County /Georgia/,* where it remained guarding the coast in that locality until the winter of 1862, when the Troop or Company was moved to the vicinity of Fort McAllister, and remained at that point during the bombardment of the fort by Federal Ironclads. The Company was then ordered to Savannah, Georgia, where, together with

*brackets indicate editorial comment

nine other troops of cavalry, the Fifth Georgia Regiment of Cavalry was formed....

After being organized the regiment was stationed at the Isle of Hope, near Savannah, Georgia, where it remained guarding the coast of that section. During this period the Federal gunboats moved up the Altamaha river, and landing at Darien /Georgia/ burned several buildings in that town, and anticipating an attempton /sic/ the part of the gunboats to ascend further up the river to Doctor Town and destroy the railroad bridge, crossing the Altamaha at that point. The Fifth squadron of the Regiment consisting of Troops "B" and "G," was detached and moved to and stationed with a battery of artillery at Barrington Ferry on the banks of the Altamaha river, about 20 miles above Darien, where they remained about six weeks. There being no further demonstration by the gunboats in that vicinity the detached sqaudron was ordered to the Isle of Hope, rejoining the regiment which was still encamped at that point. A short time after this, in the fall or winter of 1863, the regiment was called to aid in repulsing the enemy, who were advacing upon Pocatalligo, South Carolina, from the coast where they had effected a landing near Coosawhatchee, and were endeavoring to reach the railroad at that point. After the defeat of the enemy and their retiring to Port Royal, our regiment remained in that department several months, occupying positions at Pocatalligo, Adams Run, and Green Pond, South Carolina.

Our next move was to Olustee or Ocean Pond, Florida, when the Federals under General Seymore, made an attempt to reach Tallahassee, but were driven back after a crushing defeat by our Confederate troops, to their base at Jacksonville. We remained about three weeks in this department, stationed about three miles from Jacksonville. In May, 1864, the Fifth Regiment was ordered back to Savannah, and crossed the Savannah river, and following the river to Augusta, Georgia, where the regiment was put aboard cars and rushed to Atlanta, thence marched to Brush Mountain, some distance from Marietta. The Regiment was then attached to the Confederate brigade, consisting of two Alabama Regiments, two Confederate Regiments, and our Fifth Georgia Regiment. Our Colonel, R.H. Anderson, was put in command of the brigade and a short time after this he was promoted and made a brigadier general, after which the brigade was known as "Anderson's Brigade," and attached to Kelly's division, Wheeler's Corps, C.S. Cavalry, Army of North Georgia,[1] under General Joseph E. Johnston, and was actively employed in the many engagements in checking the movements of Sherman's immense army toward Atlanta. Johnston's entire force consisted of 46,000 men,[2] while Sherman commanded 196,000 men,[3] with the advantage of having superior arms, ammunition, and other military accoutrements.

Our Cavalry composed the flanks of our army and protected the rear in all retrograde movements of the army. After crossing the Chattahoochee river General Johnston had been superseded by General Hood the company actively engaged in many fights and battles around Atlanta, Jonesboro, Decatur and Newnan. Anderson's Brigade was with Wheeler and took conspicuous part in the capture of the Raiders under Federal General Stoneman, where Wheeler's Cavalry captured more than three times the number of boys in blue than he, Wheeler, had in his charging lines and columns of gray, which is an established fact of historical record.[4] On the 11th day of August, 1864, the writer's 19th birthday, General Wheeler, in obedience to an order from General Hood, then commander of chief of the army, crossed the Chattahoochee river and began operations in the rear of Sherman's Army. He succeeded in destroying a large supply of military stores, also captured a large herd of beef cattle which was driven back into our lines. On reaching Dalton we drove the garrison into their fortifications and occupied the town and destroyed considerable stores, also tore up the railroad for some distance, burning the ties and twisting the iron rails out of shape.

After leaving Dalton our march was continued into Tennessee passing through Cleveland, Athens, and Marysville, destroying stores and cutting the railroad en route. At Strawberry Plains we encountered a strong garrison occupying a fort commanding the railroad bridge which crossed the Tennessee at that point. The Fifth Georgia Regiment was here dismounted and placed in position...held the Federals in check while the balance of the command crossed the river at a ford some distance below the bridge.

Here General Wheeler divided his force, sending three brigades, consisting of Dibbrell's /Dibrell/ Tennessee Brigade, William's Kentucky Brigade and Anderson's Brigade across the Cumberland Mountains into Middle Tennessee. General Anderson, having been seriously wounded in our engagement with Stoneman's Raiders near Newnan, Georgia, General Robertson was put in charge of Anderson's Brigade during our raid through Tennessee. After crossing the Cumberland Mountains and reaching Carthage, a small village, the command halted for a short time to have our horses reshod where needed, detached parties being sent around in the neighborhood in quest of Smithies to facilitate the work. One of these parties under Captain Brailsford of the Fifth Georgia, was surprised by a scouting party of Federals and nearly the whole party were captured.

At this point General Dibbrell, with his Brigade, separated from Anderson's and William's Brigades for the purpose of gathering recruits for his command from the Southern symphathizers in that portion of the State of Tennessee.[5] Near this place Lieutenant Augustas Fleming of Company "G," Fifth Regiment, was wounded, or injured so severely that he was left with a family who kindly took care of him until he recovered. I met him since the war, and he told me that the Federals on learning of his presence, arrested him and sent him to prison, where he remained until released after the close of the war. After a stop at this place for about two days we continued on, having several brushes with bush-whackers / ambushers/ and scouting parties of Federals, our force now reduced to about 1,500 men. Our line of march was towards Mufreesboro, destroying the railroad at several points en route.

Near Murfreesboro we encountered a large force of Federal Cavalry and mounted Infantry, but held them in check long enough, it was rumored among our boys, for Gen. Robertson to stop and marry his sweetheart whom he had met at a beautiful country home, a large and spacious dwelling set in the midst of a grand park of magnificent shade trees. After the ceremony the bride in carriage, with escort and guard, took the road which we later followed towards a village called Triune. Before making this village we had a sharp brush with the enemy, who were endeavoring to rush us from the rear.

The Fifth Georgia Regiment was halted and formed in line to meet the advance, and following a rapid discharge of grape and canister into their advancing column our regiment made a counter charge upon the enemy. Colonel Bird was severely wounded just at this time, and Gen. Robertson, in the lead, shot an officer with his pistol and Lieutenant Colonel Devant ran his sabre through another officer who was leading the Federals, who were hurled back upon their reserves. The enemy soon rallied and continued the advance in full force, our command retiring slowly toward Triune. The enemy having concentrated their forces decided to make another rush, and advance their cavalry in a charge upon our line, which was retiring. General Williams, commanding the Kentucky Brigade, anticipating the movement, had dismounted his men and formed them into a line facing the approach, hidden from view. After our Regiment passed this line, the enemy, advancing rapidly, the Kentucky boys opened a destructive fire upon their advancing line, which utterly demoralized them to such an extent as to cause a hasty retreat on their part, leaving their dead and wounded on the field where they fell. Our policy was not to give battle except forced to do so, as our ammunition was limited and the purpose of our raid was to destroy as much army stores belonging to the enemy as we could locate, and cut their lines of supply and communication whenever possible to do so. We passed through Triune and on reaching Shelbyville found that the garrison that had been stationed there had hastily decamped, leaving their stores and suttler's supplies at our mercy. There as at Dalton, we gave to the citizens of the town the privilege of helping themselves to whatever they wanted and took such as we needed, and destroyed the remainder. We continued to follow the railroad lines, destroying as much as possible of the roadbed, water tanks, etc., until we arrived at a village called Sparta, where we were rejoined by Dibbrell's Tennessee Brigade, which had separated from the other two brigades, William's Kentucky and Anderson's Confederate, for the purpose of gathering up recruits from those in that section of the state of Tennessee who desired to join the regular Confederate forces, as there were several bands of what was known as partisan rangers and Southern sympathizers in that section who desired to, and did connect themselves with Dibbrell's Brigade, and continued with them until the bitter end.

After leaving this point the three reunited brigades started on their return, and as we in the ranks understood would make a rapid march to Cumberland Gap, and by concerted action with the Confederate Cavalry under Generals Morgan,[6] Duke and Vaughn, who were on the opposite side of the Gap, make /made/ a simultaneous attack at both entrances on the garrison then in possession under the command of the notorious Parson Brownlow, but on approaching the position we were to take, it was learned that General Morgan had been surprised, captured and killed by the enemy. This necessitated a change of plan on the part of our officers, for General Burbridge, in command of the Federal forces, said to number fifteen thousand men, was closely following us up, and it was necessary for our health, as well as comfort, to hunt another point at which we could cross the Cumberland Mountains. This was accomplished after an arduous fatiguing trip following the mountain roads and bridal paths, keeping a continuous skirmish with the pursuing Federals, without the loss of our train, which consisted of four rifled field howitzers, and an ambulance. After crossing the Cumberland we marched on to Bristol station, which is situated on the line of Tennessee and Virginia. We were there about two days resting, when news was received that the forces under General Burbridge, which had followed us up the mountains, had made a detour and crossed at another point, and were making for Gladesville, where our government salt works were located. Immediately our command, together with all available troops in that department, were hastened to that point, where we arrived in time to intercept the Federals and beat them back after as fierce a fight as I ever witnessed or took part in. The battle lasted about 8 o'clock a.m. until after dark. Here we came into contact for the first time with mixed troops, whites and negroes. No quarter was asked or given. That n/i/ght we rested in line of battle on top of the mountain ridge which enclosed the valley in which the salt works were located. At dawn our skirmish line, advancing, discovered that the enemy, save the dead and badly wounded, were not in our front, and upon investigation it was discovered that they had made a quiet and hasty retreat during the night. A portion of our troops were sent in pursuit, and succeeded in capturing several hundred men and horses, together with a lot of arms and ammunition. This was October, 1864, and ended the raid so far as our three brigades were concerned. General Breckenridge /Breckinridge/,[7] who commanded the troops engaged in the defense of the salt works at Gladesville, delivered an address to our three brigades commending our boys for their fortitude and gallantry during the fierce and repeated assaults made by the enemy upon our lines in their effort to capture and destroy the salt works, and that our presence in that section was opportune, as the enemy outnumbered the available troops two to one, even with our added force.

After resting a few days we took up our march headed for Georgia, crossing the Alleghaney Mountains into North Carolina, passing through Asheville, thence through the northwest portion of South Carolina to Spartanburg, crossing the Savannah river into Georgia near Abbeville, thence towards Atlanta, at that time occupied by Sherman. General Wheeler, with the other portion of his command, was in the vicinity of Newnan, Georgia, and immediately after consolidation we struck Sherman's army at Bear Creek station, and had a desperate encounter with the enemy's infantry, losing about one-third of our regiment in killed, wounded and captured. I think our officers were deceived as to the number of the enemy at that point, and dismounted our men to hold a certain position on the railroad, and held the position too long with such a small force. The enemy attacked in such overwhelming force that our boys were run over and cut to pieces before they could be reinforced. One of our color guards, T.Q. Fleming of Company G, was one of those who succeeded in making their escape, and gave a thrilling account of his experience. He stated that just as they were closing in on our line a riderless horse from the enemy's side dashed up to our lines. He succeeded in getting hold of the bridle reign and brought the horse to a halt. He then mounted him and attempted to assist color bearer, Sergeant Russell Walthour, to mount also, but was so hard pressed that he failed. He took the colors from Walthour and succeeded in making his escape, winning the race by a close shave. About two hundred yards to the rear of this point a heavier line was formed in reserve and checked a further advance of the enemy. Our color bearer on discovering that he was left threw himself down on the ground. The enemy, thinking he was dead, passed him by. Fortunately, there was a clump of bushes nearby, into which he crawled and secreted himself until dark, when he succeeded in getting to cover in the woods nearby, slipping through the enemy's line, and regained our lines in safety, just as we were going into camp near Griffin, Georgia. For several days before reaching Macon we were continuously engaged skirmishing with the Federal Cavalry, commanded by General Kilpatrick,[8] and succeeded in forcing them to keep near their infantry support, thereby saving a great deal of property from being destroyed by bands of their foraging parties and marauders, confining the district through which Sherman passed as narrow a trail as possible. When we reached Macon, General Hardee had gathered up a small force, too small and feeble to make any resistance to Sherman's hosts, but aided in preventing an entrance into Macon. We had a brush with the enemy at Griswoldville[9] and succeeded in forcing him to keep in close columns and in touch one with another, thereby preventing them from overrunning a wider stretch of territory, thus saving much property of our people from destruction. The Georgia home guards,[10] or state troops, composed of men too old and boys too young to serve in the army, took part in this fight, and it was said of them, that they were a band of heroes and knew not the meaning of the word "Retreat," but held their ground like the Old Guards, with few their equals and none their superiors, in gallantry and brave resistance, while facing the charging battle line of Sherman's well trained and seasoned soldiers. All honor to the Gallant Home Guards, many of whom were martyrs that day. Braver men or boys never lived or died than they.

General Hardee, with his small force, fell back towards Savannah, doing what he could in obstructing Sherman's progress in that direction, while General Wheeler with his cavalry guarded the approaches to Augusta. He had an engagement at Waynesboro and Brier Creek, driving Kilpatrick's cavalry back to their infantry columns and continued to harass Sherman's flanks and rear until reaching some distance below Augusta, when he crossed his command over the Savannah river, and resisted successfully Sherman's efforts to cross over any portion of his troops to the Carolina side for the purpose of cutting off the retreat of the small force that General Hardee had collected, and were occupying the fortifications in and around the city of Savannah. Hardee evacuated the city the 24th of December, 1864, crossing the Savannah river on pontoon bridges to the Carolina side and moved up the coast.

Soon Sherman resumed his advance through Carolina. About this time General Wheeler was reinforced by Butler's Brigade, which had been detached from Hampton's Cavalry in Virginia. Sherman, continuing to advance, we had daily brushes and skirmishes with Kilpatrick's Cavalry and the mounted infantry adjuncts of the Infantry Corps.

At Aiken, Kilpatrick made an attempt to enter the village. Wheeler set a trap for him, forming his command in shape of the letter "V," extending with top towards the approach; side lines on each side of road, and bottom of letter at Aiken. Iverson's Brigade occupied the center of approach, facing Kilpatrick's advancing column, with instructions to fall back towards Aiken, drawing the enemy in between our two extended lines, which at the proper time would close in upon their column from either side, but Iverson failed to give way fast enough, and our lines were discovered, and the plan was a partial failure. The enemy turned around and made a hasty retreat, losing several hundred men and horses killed, wounded and captured, besides part of one of their batteries captured from them when our boys closed in on them from both flanks. This taught Kilpatrick a lesson which I don't think he ever forgot, for never thereafter did he leave the main infantry column for any distance, but continued in easy reach.

After repulsing the enemy at Aiken, S.C., driving back their cavalry under General Kilpatrick to their infantry column, which was headed for Columbia, our Cavalry took up a line of march parallel to the same point. It was a very cold day and night, rain and sleet falling steadily on us as we marched in column en route, everything covered with ice, icicles hanging from our hat rims and stirrup guards. The manes, tails and fetlocks /above and behind the hoof/ of our horses were frozen, and a bridge we crossed had to be sanded continuously to enable our horses to keep their feet while mounting and descending the slopes at either end.

It was sometime after night before we halted and went into camp for the rest of the night. We soon had big fires burning, and after drying our clothes and warming we wrapped up in our blankets and lay down by the fires to get what rest and sleep we could. At dawn we were up and by sunrise we were again in our saddles and on the march. Our Regiment, the 5th Georgia, headed our column, and shortly after leaving our camping ground we were passing a field on our right, enclosed with a rail fence, which was about thirty feet from the road, and on the fence were perched about two dozen soldier boys wrapped in their regulation overcoats, enjoying the warm rays of the sun, which felt good after our experience of the day and night just preceding.

I will here state that the majority of our boys wore over their uniforms either rubber ponchos or the United States army overcoat of blue, involuntarily supplied by the boys in blue. The boys on the fence had left their arms in their camp, and, as usual, chaffing began between them and the boys on the march, but all at once a discovery was made which caused the boys on the fence to fall off like so many cooters of a log in a mill pond, and scoot like wild turkeys for the other side of the field. The discovery was mutual, but before any shots were fired at the fleeing Yanks some big-hearted "Johnny" among us called out in a loud voice: "Don't shoot them boys, they haven't any arms—let them go." The Yanks, on reaching the other side of the field, looked around at us, and it appearing that no effort was being made by any of us to pursue them, and no shots were fired at them, they stopped, waved their hats to us, and leisurely entered the woods beyond, rejoining their comrades. Evidently we had camped within a hundred yards or so of each other during the night under the impression that we were part and parcel of the same command.

We continued our march toward Columbia, parallel to the enemy's line, and at noon had a brush with their infantry. A part of our Cavalry took a road to the left, leading as I understand to Lexington, and my recollection is that it was General William's Kentucky Brigade. We continued our march, but the position of Anderson's Brigade was changed from the head to the rear of the column, and did not cross the river at Columbia until late that night, and I think we crossed below the city, over a railroad bridge temporarily planked over for the occasion, and marched through and camped on the outskirts of the city on the north side. Next morning we were moved back and across the river, over a covered bridge, and took position to the right, some distance from the bridge. We understood that we were there for the purpose of guarding the approaches to the bridge and protecting the flank of William's Brigade, which was coming through from Lexington and were headed for and were expected to cross at that bridge. General Joseph Wheeler (our Little Joe) was with General R. H. Anderson and his Brigade when we crossed and took position over on the west side of the river, to the right of the bridge, and when William's Kentucky Brigade came to where we were stationed, General Wheeler directed the movements in crossing at the bridge, and I think our (Anderson's) Brigade brought up the rear and crossed after the Kentucky Brigade. At any rate the bridge, a covered one, was on fire when we got to it and a number of our men were trying to extinguish the flames, using water from barrels that were on each side of the passageway the length of the bridge, and succeeded in checking the fire sufficiently to allow our troops to cross. Several of our men and horses were severely scorched, however, and a squad of six or eight were unable to force their horses to enter the bridge, and had to turn back and followed the river up until they succeeded in finding a crossing.

They rejoined the command about a week later after being given up as lost. Our command after crossing moved to the right across a stretch of meadow, toward what appeared to be large factory buildings, passing on our left a body of cavalry in line and facing our flank as we moved in column. I understand that this was General Butler's command, a part of General Hampton's Cavalry. Shortly after taking position near the river bank, the enemy with a battery of howitzers began to shell that portion of the city and got our range. We were then moved further back and a portion of our men were dismounted and were deployed along the bank of the river, where they remained until driven out by the enemy, who had crossed the river somewhere below and entered the city, of which fact we were not long in ignorance, for Sherman soon had his beacon lights started and bond fires aglow, leaving a pathway of devastation and destruction back to the Savannah river, thence through Georgia to Atlanta.

This condition continued until we reached North Carolina. Fragments of Hood's army had been coming in and General Joseph E. Johnston was put in command of the remnant of infantry and artillery that had once been the grand army of North Georgia. For though diminutive compared with its opponent, the Federal army under Sherman, no individual who was connected with this army while under General Johnston but knows that no troops at any time had greater confidence in their chief than did the army of North Georgia in Joseph E. Johnston. They were ready at all times to do or die at his command, and our confidence was not misplaced.

After taking command, General Johnston got his troops together and the spirits of the men seemed to revive. We were not whipped yet by a long shot. Skirmishing was of a daily occurrence. At Fayetteville our Cavalry surprised and captured a number of Kilpatrick's men and missed by a small margin this festive gentleman himself, but did get his companion and personal outfit.[11]

At Bentonville Johnston exhibited his military ability and scored his last victory. With a force of not over fifteen thousand men he held in check and repulsed charge after charge and assault after assault made by troops numbering almost ten to one, who were flushed with victory, having made a triumphal march through hostile country several hundred miles almost unopposed.[12]

They, with surprising step and sparkling eye, the veteran of a hundred battles, with undoubting faith in victory already won, charged upon this small array of boys in gray tatters, who stood unprotected by bank or rock, with nerves of steel and bated breath. When at the command to fire each volley told its tale, foe like standing grain before the harvest blade the advancing line went down in death. And as the sun sank low the battle ceased and night approaching drew her mantle over the scene, thus hiding from view the gruesome sight, the ground now strewn with blood-stained and mangled forms, some our friends and comrades and others our foes, for both the blue and gray lay wounded, dead, or dying out there between our lines.

The army surgeons and hospital corps were soon busy attending the wounded upon the field, while our boys sought rest after the fatigues of the day.

Early next day our Cavalry was moved toward Smithfield, where we encountered the enemy's cavalry, and skirmishing continued daily.

But the end was near. Soon we heard the sad tidings—Lee had surrendered. It was hard to believe the message, but soon we were convinced of the truth of the report, for soon small squads of men in ragged gray uniforms came straggling by and confirmed the sad, sad news—Lee had surrendered. I saw strong men shed tears on that day, but not of shame—for well they knew that all that man could do they had done.

Fortunately General Grant was a true soldier and could appreciate an honorable and valiant foe, and agreed to terms of surrender that of a right we were entitled to, and each soldier was allowed to retain possession of his personal property. The Cavalrymen had furnished their own horses, but most of us had United States saddles and bridles, but no question was raised about that, so we retained them also.

Our infantry was at Greensboro and the Cavalry under Wheeler was at a place called Company shops, and between our infantry and the Federal army at the time of surrender of Johnston's army, which was on the 26th day of April, 1865....

After the surrender we started on our return to our homes in Georgia, and after arriving at Augusta we separated in small parties, each selecting the most direct route. I arrived at Tebeauville, Ware county, where our family had refugeed, rejoining them after an absence of three years, May, 1862-May, 1865.

Notes:

[1] Commonly known as the Army of Tennessee.

[2] Johnston's force during the Atlanta campaign is listed as 55,306 effectives as of April 30, 1864. Livermore, Thomas L. *Numbers and Losses in the Civil War in America*. (Cambridge: The University Press, 1901), 119. On April 30, 1864, Johnston listed his total strength at 52,992 "present for duty" while Major E.C. Davis of the 53rd Ohio Regiment lists Johnston's force at 55,000. *Battles*

and Leaders of the Civil War, 4 vols. (1887; reprint, Secaucus, NY: Castle, n.d.), vol. IV, 281.

[3] Livermore lists Sherman's strength on April 30, 1864, as 110,123 effectives. *Numbers and Losses*, 119. Sherman lists his force as close to 100,000 strong. *Battles and Leaders*, vol. IV, 252.

[4] This is commonly referred to as Stoneman's Raid. During the Atlanta campaign the Confederate cavalry was still superior to their Federal counterparts in every aspect except weaponry. Consequently, the Federal cavalry was largely ineffective against Wheeler's Confederate troopers. General Sherman lost confidence in his cavalry corps and assigned them to duty as auxiliary infantry. Yet on July 27, 1864, he gave his cavalry one last chance to redeem themselves and sent them to sever General Hood's remaining supply lines. Federal General George Stoneman took 6,500 Federal cavalry and headed east of Atlanta, while General Edward McCook, along with 3,500 troopers, headed west. They were to meet at Lovejoy's station to sever the last remaining railroad into Confederate controlled Atlanta. Their secondary objective was to precede to Macon then to Andersonville and secure the release of 30,000 Federal prisoners of war. Stoneman opted instead to make Macon his first target. As a result, the Confederate cavalry handed the Federals a crushing defeat. Stoneman and over 700 Federal cavalry were captured by Confederate forces and imprisoned with the very men they had intended to free.

Lambright places Anderson's brigade and the 5th Georgia Cavalry with the Confederate force pursuing General Stoneman, but Wheeler's report, October 9, 1864, states that the Confederates spilt their force. Wheeler sent Iverson's, Allen's, and Breckinridge's brigades to intercept Stoneman's cavalry. Wheeler took part of Jackson's division, plus Ashby's and Anderson's brigades to confront McCook. Nonetheless, the Confederate horseman badly cut up the Federals and McCook barely escaped capture. Both generals, Stoneman and McCook, once again failed to meet Sherman's expectations.

[5] Though Tennessee seceded from the Union, she did not go easily. Union sentiment was particularly strong in the eastern part of the state, and Unionists tried to break away and create a separate state—East Tennessee. Tennessee contributed greatly to the Union

war effort. Close to 40,000 men from the state served in the Federal army. See Current, Richard Nelson. *Lincoln's Loyalist: Union Soldiers from the Confederacy.* (New York: Oxford University Press, 1994), 215.

[6] Confederate General John Hunt Morgan was a daring and innovative cavalry commander who operated primarily in Tennessee and Kentucky. He conducted a number of raids in both states, as well as a 24 day daring raid through Indiana and Ohio. His Ohio raid left a swath of destruction where he demolished bridges, damaged railroads and captured 6,000 Federal troops. He was finally captured at the end of his raid and imprisoned in Ohio but soon escaped. Morgan was mortally wounded in an engagement in Tennessee on September 4, 1864.

[7] John Breckinridge, former Vice President of the United States (1856-1861), was a presidential nominee on the split Democratic ticket in 1860. This split allowed Lincoln and the Republican party to win the presidency with a minority of the popular vote. As vice president, Breckinridge resided over the joint session of congress that declared the election of Abraham Lincoln as president. Breckinridge was soon elected to the senate by the state of Kentucky and was a strong voice against Lincoln's war policy which, consequently, resulted in an order for his arrest in September, 1861. He fled Washington, though he had committed no treasonous act, and was appointed as a Brigadier General in the Confederate Army. Soon he was promoted to Major General and distinguished himself in battle as a corps commander.

[8] Major General Judson Kilpatrick commanded a cavalry division under General Sherman during Sherman's push toward Atlanta but was wounded. He recovered, resumed command and rejoined Sherman on his march through Georgia and the Carolinas. Kilpatrick was also Joseph Wheeler's former West Point classmate. A bitter exchange of words erupted between the two cavalry leaders as they continually clashed and skirmished. General Wheeler blamed General Kilpatrick for needless depradations committed against the southern populace, but Kilpatrick blamed Wheeler's beleaguered troops for depradations against their own citizens. Wheeler started the correspondence, "Since the commencement of this sad war I have used untiring efforts to maintain in my soldiers

principles of chivalry and true soldiery honor. They have been taught to despise and spurn the cowardly instincts which induce low men to frighten, abuse, and rob defenseless women and children.... I have only to ask, for the sake of these old associations, for your own sake, and for the sake of the institution where military honor was taught, that you will offer some protection to the families left defenseless, and not leave them at the mercy of a brutal soldiery."

Wheeler to Kilpatrick, December 5, 1864, *The War of the Rebellion: A compilation of the Official Records of the Union and Confederate Armies*, 70 vols. in 128 parts, ser. 1, vol. XLIV, 635. (Hereafter cited as *Official Records*)

Kilpatrick was quick to reply, "I will simply say that the same complaints have been made by the citizens of Georgia against your officers and men of your own command. If you cannot control your men while they are among their friends, you cannot expect me to control my men from committing depradations upon their own enemies...."

Kilpatrick to Wheeler, December 13, 1864, *Ibid.*, 706.

Yet, Wheeler's claims were certainly justified. The records are filled with senseless deeds committed by Union soldiers that far exceeded military justification. After the war, Kilpatrick was quoted in reference to his march through Georgia and the Carolinas, "When travelers passing through South Carolina shall see chimney stacks without houses, and the country desolate, and shall ask, 'Who did this?' some Yankee shall answer Kilpatrick's cavalry."

⁹ Griswoldville, Georgia, was the site of a Confederate munitions factory that produced brass framed copies of the Colt 1851 Navy revolver, a favorite of officers and cavalrymen. On November 20, 1864, Sherman's forces destroyed the factory; it was never rebuilt.

¹⁰ The Georgia militia suffered 523 casualties during their engagement on November 22, 1864, and were described as being "badly cut up." Yet, they kept close contact with the enemy until dark. For an excellent account see "The Georgia Militia during Sherman's March to the Sea," by Gustavus W. Smith, Major-General, C.S.A., *Battles and Leaders of the Civil War*, IV, 667-669.

¹¹ On the morning of March 10, 1865, General Wheeler's cavalry charged into Kilpatrick's camp and surprised their Federal

counter parts. "In less than a minute," Kilpatrick later wrote, "They had driven back my people, and taken possession of my headquarters, captured the artillery, and the whole command was flying before the most formidable cavalry charge I ever witnessed.... Colonel Spencer and a large portion of my staff were virtually taken prisoner."

Kilpatrick's report, April 5, 1865, *Official Records.*, ser. 1, vol. XLVII, pt.1, 861.

In fact, Kilpatrick was forced to flee in his night clothes. Some writers claim that Wheeler's men presented him with Kilpatrick's horse and pistols from the raid.

[12] The battle of Bentonville was one of the last attempts of the Confederate army to show its once mighty strength, yet they were simply overwhelmed by the numerical superiority of their enemy. Preparations for the battle began as the remnant of the Army of Tennessee straggled into North Carolina; they were quickly joined by General Hardee's command and General Wheeler's and General Wade Hampton's cavalry corps, as well as small bands of Confederate forces from the area. On the eve of the battle General Johnston and his officers held a council of war. Two possibilities were suggested: The first, to march the newly combined force of approximately 20,000 men to Virginia to aid General Robert E. Lee in defense against General Ulysses S. Grant. The second possibility, which was adopted by Johnston, though not all were in consent, was to strike a pre-emptive blow against Sherman's left wing commanded by General Henry W. Slocum. Their objective was to cripple Slocum's column before Sherman could provide reinforcements, which were one day's march away, thus impeding Sherman from reaching Virginia and to prolong or prevent Sherman's forces from reaching and combining forces with General Grant. Indeed, it was a hotly contested battle, and the first day saw much bloodletting as Johnston's forces struck hard against the Federal jugular. But, Slocum was reinforced by the end of the second day and Johnston's forces had to retire. Soon, the end for Lee, Johnston and the whole of the Confederacy came to fruition.

The infantry forces under Johnston were about 14,000, but they operated as three separate groups and never consolidated, by the second day of battle they were pitted against Sherman's 60,000 men.

The Antagonists: Wheeler, Sherman, Johnston

Joseph Wheeler
Joseph Wheeler (1836-1906) graduated from the United States Military Academy in 1859 and received his commission as second lieutenant in the U.S. Army. He served two years with the U.S. Cavalry in Missouri and New Mexico and gained experience fighting Indians. When the Civil War broke out in 1861 he resigned his commission and was given a commission in the Confederate States Army. He quickly rose from lieutenant to colonel and helped Braxton Bragg prepare defenses at the captured Federal fort at Pensacola, Florida.

Wheeler served conspicuously at the battle of Shiloh (April 1862), and later the same year was promoted to general and given command of the cavalry forces of the Army of the Mississippi. He earned a reputation as an excellent commander and vivacious fighter. He served with Bragg in the Kentucky campaign (Aug.-Oct. 1862) and gained notoriety covering Bragg's retreating army that would earn his place in military history. Wheeler saw action at the battle of Stone's River (Jan. 1863) where he joined forces with and commanded Nathan Bedford Forrest. The two cavalry commanders exchanged heated words and had many differences of opinion, and would never serve together again. Wheeler fought at the Confederate victory at Chickamauga (Aug.-Sept. 1863) and committed one of the most notorious cavalry raids of the war during the Chattanooga campaign (Oct.-Nov. 1863), destroying nearly everything in his path and terrorizing Federal troops. He also fought with General James Longstreet at Knoxville (Nov.-Dec. 1863).

Wheeler commanded the cavalry forces of the Army of Tennessee during the Atlanta Campaign (May-Sept. 1864) and his was the only force to battle Sherman on the Federal march through Georgia (Nov.-Dec. 1864) and the Carolinas (Jan.-April 1865).

After the war, the 5' 5" spunky little fighter turned his energies to politics and was elected to Congress by the state of Alabama where he served from 1880-1898. He became known as a gifted politician and orator and chaired the House Ways and Means Committee from 1894-1898.

When war with Spain loomed in 1898, President William McKinley appointed Wheeler as major general of United States volunteer forces. The appointment was hailed throughout the nation as a healing of the wounds of the Civil War. Newspaper headlines read:

"BLUE AND GRAY UNITED." "FIGHTIN' JOE TO FIGHT AGAIN." "GRIZZLED JOE WHEELER DRAWS HIS SWORD AGAIN."

Wheeler was given command of the cavalry of the American expeditionary force that would sail to Cuba to battle the Spanish. One of the regiments under Wheeler's command was the First U.S. Volunteer Cavalry, better known as the "Rough Riders," commanded by Theodore Roosevelt. Wheeler saw action in the first fighting against Spanish regulars in Cuba during the Santiago expedition, and also at the battle of San Juan Hill.

After Cuba fell to American forces, Wheeler briefly served with General Arthur McArthur (father of Douglas McArthur) in the Philippines from August 1899 to January 1900. Later that same year he retired from public life.

Wheeler died while visiting his sister in Brooklyn on January 26, 1906. The one time West Point cadet, Indian fighter, Confederate commander, politician, and major general of U.S. forces had finally met his match. He was given a military parade through the streets of Manhattan. From Manhattan his body was carried to Washington D.C., where it lay in state at St. John's Episcopal Church. Both Confederate and Union veterans, as well as Spanish-American War veterans formed the procession that followed Wheeler's body to the cemetery. He was buried in Arlington National Cemetery.

Willam Tecumseh Sherman

Hated by the South (and still vilified by many southerners over 100 years later) and loved (for the most part) by the North, William Tecumseh Sherman was and is an enigma.

Sherman graduated sixth in his 1840 West Point class. Later in life he remarked that the academy was ill prepared to instruct students for real war. But, who could have foreseen the destruction that would one day come from the hand of the slender cadet.

After graduation from West Point, Sherman's first assignment was in the South, a place and people he would come to admire. When hostilities erupted at Fort Sumter in 1861 Sherman was headmaster of the Louisiana State Seminary and Military Academy, the forerunner of Louisiana State University. In fact, early in the war, Sherman was offered a high rank in the newly formed Rebel army.

Sherman saw action at Bull Run (Manassas) where his brigade suffered inglorious defeat, Shiloh, Memphis, Vicksburg, Chattanooga, the Atlanta Campaign, The March to the Sea, and the Carolinas Campaign.

His favorite quote, "war is hell," was not original, though most attribute him with the phrase. His total war against the civilian populace was unheard of in mid-nineteenth century, Victorian America, and he received criticism from both North and South alike for his destruction. Yet, he hastened the end of the war, and brought the war home to the untouched heart of Dixie.

There are varying theories of what promoted him to issue Special Field Order 120: "Forage liberally. A devastation. More or less relentless..." that devastated much of Georgia and South Carolina. After the fall of Vicksburg, Sherman's family came to stay with him and it was here, in the Mississippi swamps, that the darling of his life, his youngest son, nine year old "Little Wille" succumbed to typhoid and soon died. Sherman and his family were devastated.

Did Sherman, a one time friend and admirer of the South, husband, and devoted father issue Special Field Order 120 for military reasons only, to avenge the Union, or to avenge the death of his youngest son? Only he will ever know.

Joseph E. Johnston

Joseph E. Johnston was the only commander to have the distinction of commanding both the Army of Northern Virginia and the Army of Tennessee, the two main fighting forces of the Confederacy. He was a competent general and loved by his soldiers.

When Johnston replaced General Braxton Bragg as the commander of the Army of Tennessee the morale of the demoralized troops increased dramatically, desertion stopped, and those who had left the ranks, frustrated with Bragg's harsh treatment, returned. A soldier in Johnston's army made the following comment: "When the news came, like pouring oil upon the troubled waters, that General Joe E. Johnston of Virginia had taken command of the Army of Tennessee, men returned to their companies, order was restored... He was loved, respected, admired; yea, almost worshipped by his troops. I do not believe there was a soldier in his army but would gladly have died for him. With him everything was his soldiers, and the newspapers, criticizing him at the time, said, 'He would feed his soldiers if the country starved.' ...We soon got proud, the blood of the old Cavaliers tingled in our veins..."

Unfortunately for Johnston and the Confederacy, the general and Jefferson Davis often disagreed and eventually developed an adversarial relationship. Johnston's defense of Atlanta was arguably a master piece of defensive strategy, but his skill was unrecognized in Richmond and he lost command of the army that he had so diligently worked to improve.

Johnston graduated from West Point in 1829 and was commissioned as second lieutenant in the artillery where he remained until 1836. Later he was promoted to captain and then to lieutenant colonel. He fought in the Mexican War (1847) and served under General Winfield Scott. He was severely wounded in fighting around Cerro Gordo.

After the war with Mexico Johnston served in the Topographical Engineers, and on June 28, 1860, was promoted to quartermaster general and finally brigadier general.

Johnston commanded Confederate forces at First Bull Run (Manassas), during the Peninsula Campaign (Spring 1862), and Seven Pines (May 3-June 1, 1863), where he was wounded and command of the Army of Northern Virginia was given to Robert E. Lee.

After recuperating, Johnston was placed in command of the Army of the Mississippi and saw limited action at Vicksburg (July 1863). On December 27, 1863, he was placed in command of the Army of Tennessee to try to stop Sherman's massive offensive in

North Georgia. He was replaced by General John Bell Hood on July 17, 1864, and didn't receive a command again until General Lee, now commander of all Confederate forces, placed Johnston in the field to consolidate forces to stop Sherman from moving through North Carolina into Virginia. His last battle was at Bentonville, North Carolina, on March 19-21, 1865, and on April 26 he signed the conditions of surrender set by Sherman.

After the war Johnston opened an insurance business in Savannah, which is still in operation. Later, he served in the U.S. House of Representatives from the commonwealth of Virginia (1879-1881), (1885-1891). His memoirs, Narrative of *Military Operations During the Late War Between the States*, was published in 1874. He became friends with his old nemesis, W.T. Sherman, and served as his pall bearer (February 14, 1891). Yet, fate would have her irony, and Johnston caught pneumonia from a rain storm at Sherman's funeral. Five weeks later he died. A braver and truer soldier there never was.

4

Confederate War Vignettes

The following account by a veteran's wife, four letters written by soldiers during the war, and a battle account reflect the wide range of sentiment toward the war. Some saw it as exciting and endured its hardships well, while others chaffed under its yoke. Whatever one's inclination or particular bias toward the war may be, all must surely agree that it was, indeed, a time that tried our nation's very soul. Fortunately, out of the hardships and ashes of war, a new and stronger nation emerged. One that would rise to the global stage as a major player, first, during the Spanish American War in 1898 and again during World War I, and establish herself as the guardian of freedom. Perhaps in this light and in this hope the enormous loss of life and tremendous tragedy can be justified.

A. Reminiscences of a Veteran's Wife
When the war between the states broke out I was just a young girl, 16 years of age. My father Nicholas Stregles lived over Briar Creek, at a place called Tukahoe /?/ it was in the fork of Briar Creek, and the Savannah River.

We were not disturbed very much by the enemy, because they found out that this was the spot of the 'Battle of Briar Creek,' / Brier/ fought during the Revolutionary war, and remembering the result, they passed on by,[1] however there were a few straglers /sic/

42

who ventured in; and of these was captured by one of our confederate soldiers, for they were in camp over there guarding the bridges to keep the enemy from crossing over into South Carolina.

The one captured was a young man, a mere boy, one of the soldiers took him up on his horse behind him, and rode around the neighborhood telling the people to come and look at him, for he wanted them to see a Yankee. I was sorry for him, and said to the soldier don't hurt him for I know his mother is worried about him this minute. The farmers over in there went right on with their farms raising fine crops of corn, sugar cane potatoes and live stock hogs, cows etc. Now when Sherman's army passed through Effingham County,[2] 'which is just below Screven,' and destroyed every thing in their path, the people there were in danger of starving, They heard about these people ove/r/ Briar Creek having corn and meat to spare they came to buy, even some women whose husbands and sons were in the army would come, and go back, with a bushel of corn and a side of meat saying we have been to Egypt to buy corn.

At this time the Brian's and the Brannons bridges had both been burned, by the Confederate Soldiers to keep the enemy from crossing over into South Carolina. So these people had no way to get across, but were met at the creek by the residents, who took the provisions across to them in boats. The men who owned these farms, were a Mr. Waters, Mr. John Kittles, Mr. Micklebury Williamson, he was a rich man, and my father Nicholas Stregles, his father, my grand-father was Captain Nicolas Stregles, of the Revolutionary war. My mother was Miss Eliza McQueen. I was born Dec. 29, 1844, at old Jacksonboro/./ I dont remember, just how old, but when a small girl, we moved over /B/riar Creek, at a placed called Shumake, about 5 miles from black Creek Church. I joined the Methodist Church at old Union in May 1861/./ moved my membership to Buck Creek church, in 1871, where it is at the present time, I was married to James Robert Lee, Dec. 24, 1868.

I am now 85 years of age. I live with my son Frank Lee near Halcyondale, Ga."

Mrs. Louisianna Lee,
Sept. 14th 1929.

B. A brave color-bearer

The following story was written by Mrs. Atwood, wife of Captain Atwood of the 5th Georgia Cavalry, included in *Biographical and Military sketch of William Michael Henderson*, Georgia Department of Archives and History.

The incident occurred when Wheeler's troops, including the 5th Georgia Cavalry, were following Sherman on his march to Savannah and engaged General Kilpatrick's cavalry at Waynesboro, Georgia.

The battle of Waynesboro took place as Federal forces reached south Georgia. The engagements took place on November 27 and 28, 1864 and consisted of cavalry under Judson Kilpatrick and Confederate cavalry under Joseph Wheeler. During two days of skirmishing Wheeler's forces halted the Federals and soundly defeated their counterpart. On December 4 the Confederate cavalry again engaged Federal cavalry in heavy fighting that lasted throughout the day. Both sides fought ferociously but by the end of the day the Federals managed to drive the Rebel troopers from several positions. Kilpatrick was helped greatly, if not saved, by Federal infantry that came to his rescue. Both sides claimed victory that day, but it was only a side show to the reality of Sherman and his thunderous march to the sea.[3]

The beginning of the story is symbolic of the sentiment paid to those veterans who lived long enough for their war records to become living legend to a new generation of southerners who honored and deeply respected these aged warriors who had worn gray and butternut.

A Brave color-bearer

An incident of conspicuous daring is told of W.M. Henderson of the Cavalry Troop which, with the 'McIntosh Cavalry' formed the fifth squadron of the 5th Ga. Regt. of Cavalry. This young man, almost a boy in years, but endowed with all the heroic valor of his southern ancestry, was acting flag-bearer of his brigade, when the brigade over-powered by numbers, was retreating in hot haste, he, inspired with the courage born of a just cause, stopped, and turning his horse to face the enemy, used his flag staff as a weapon with which he dismounted the adjutant of the 9th Michigan Regiment, capturing him and his horse and bridle and saddle, two fine army revolvers, sabre and belt. The sabre belt was a very fine one, much nicer than any used in our Army, and was given a trophy to Gen. R.H. Anderson. The Yankees were repulsed and young Henderson was handed next morning a promotion for "Brilliant and conspicuous bravery on the field of battle."

C. War time letters of Bernard C. Wagner
5th Georgia Cavalry
The following letters were written by Lieutenant Wagner during the Atlanta campaign to his cousin Emmie (who probably lived in south Georgia). It is an example of the close family ties that existed during the war, particularly between soldiers and female family members. It is said that Confederate women kept the war alive even after the inevitable was obvious. It is they who often encouraged and continually stirred the flames of devotion and patriotism in their soldiers.

Part of the second letter is unintelligible due to age and wear. Both letters contain numerous grammatical errors.

Camp — 2 miles from Atlanta June 3 1864
Dear Emmie,
I drop you this to let you know that I am well, but seeing hard times in this part of the Globe, we have the Yankees about ten miles from us, we hear the artillery of both sides every day, and I expect in a few days a large battle will take place between Johns/t/ on on our side & Sherman on the other, in this camp we have about five thousand men, and plenty of guns and ammunition for them, I do not know when we will move, but I dont think we will stay here long, at this camp I mean, if Johns/t/on has to fall back we will go to reinforce him, I spent a very hard night of it last night and yesterday for we had a very heavy rain & got all my blankets wet and also myself, Everything was drenched in this camp. I must close, give my love to all the family and write soon.
Your Affectionate Cousin Bernard

Battery near Atlanta July 8

Dear Emmie,

it is with great pleasure I rec'd your welcome letter a few days ago and I now hasten to reply. You will think it is any thing else but /?/, it is certainly so, as the Yankees would not give us much time to waste. The Yankees commenced shelling us on the morning of the 8th of July and continued for three days and nights, but thank God only two slightly wounded, they sent at their /?/ of one hundred shells a day, there was hardly a tree anywhere about us but was not torn in splinters. One night before last we were ordered to take charge of a Battery within two miles of this city, we had to march twelve miles that night, we started at night 1'OClock and reached the battery. At 2 O'clock in the morning, traveling over one of these moist roads that is in the country the mud being in some places up to our knees and every /?/ of a mile we had to go in the mud to push the Cannon and as the horses could not move them, the night before we left we had one of the most beautiful fights that mortal can ever see it was an artillery duel and lasted three hours, the duel took place on the bank of the bloody Chattahoochee where many poor fellows had laid down their life for his country. General Johnston had fallen back and is within eight miles of the city where he has made a stand and intends to hold it at any cost. Most all the places of business in and around Atlanta are shut off and the inhabitants are leaving in large numbers, Every train of cars that are in /?/ city are as full as they can be. It is a very hard sight to see the fine country /?/ with out any protection save that of the destructive soldiers. Well Emma I must close give my love to all the family and /?/

From your affectionate cousin,

Bernard

P.S.

before I close I will give you evidence of /?/

Bill of fare for 2nd Bat heavy Artillery

Friday July 8th 1864.

1/3 Round rotten Bacon

1 /?/ meal Per day

1 ounce Salt

D. The misgivings of a soldier

The following story was found in a copy of a Ludawici, Georgia newspaper, dated June 8, 1967. It is a wartime letter written by Thomas Wayman Houston to his brother James. Thomas W. Houston initially enlisted in the Altamaha Scouts, Company I, 25th Georgia Regiment. Later he joined company K of the 5th Georgia Cavalry. The letter to his brother, one of sadness and misgivings about the Confederate cause, was written from Green Pond, S.C. a few months before the 5th Georgia Cavalry was dispatched to north Georgia to participate in the Atlanta Campaign.

Dear Brother:

I have just received your kind letter and I was glad to hear that you were all well. I am as well as common. I have no news worth your attention, only I think that our people are about to give up Charleston[4] for I see that they are moving a great many of the cannons out on the railroad. The Yankees have taken John's Island since we left it. They killed one or two men and wounded six or seven and took eight horses and two guns. You talk about gaining our independence. I can't see any chance for it for our men are too demoralized. And this regiment is not alone for it is so everywhere I can hear from. The Yankees have completely got us in their power and they can subjugate us in a short time and never fire another gun for they soon can starve us out. They have got Tennessee and Kentucky completely cut off from us and you know it will be impossible for the state of South Carolina and Georgia to feed our soldiers. I don't see what our Congress is doing that they don't try for peace on some terms.[5] I think that they might come on some terms that would be honorable on both sides. I can tell you if they don't do something pretty soon the men will do it for them. I believe these big officers will carry on the war just as long as they can. As for my part, I am tired of it, being half starved and our horses dying. I think if they can't do any better they had better quit and let the men go home and make something for their families to live on. As for the Yankees making slaves of us, I don't believe they will ever do that, for Lincoln, in his last proclamation says that if we will come back into the Union, that he will guarantee to us all the rights of property excepting slaves and I think he would do a great deal better than that if our men would try for it. Oh, James, I never wanted to see home so bad in my life as I do now and there is no telling when I ever will get the chance to go there. I do hope this War will end soon. I want you and William to be sure and hire a hand for Esther for if you don't, I don't see what she is to do. There is no chance for me to help her where I am for it takes all our wages to buy something to eat. I think it is a very hard case that the Government can't feed her soldiers, but I need not say anymore about that. I want you and William to see to my hogs and mark the pigs for me and if I ever get the chance I will do the same for you.... I must come to a close. You must write soon and let me know all the news about there. So, nothing more, but I remain your brother. T.W. Houston.

P.S. Do send this letter to Esther as soon as you can. H.W. C.

Thomas died at the battle of Kennesaw seven months after he wrote this letter. Ironically, it was a Confederate victory.

E. Hardtimes in Florida

The following letter was written by Henry Greene Edenfield to his wife, Jane. Edenfield served in the Confederate army from 1862-1865. Edenfield wrote his letter just a few months before the 5th Georgia Cavalry was dispatched to Atlanta. True to his convictions, he survived the war and lived into the next century. This letter also contains numerous spelling and grammatical errors.

Camp Finigan State of Florida

March 12th 1864

My Dear Wife

I will take the opportunity of writing you a few lines which I hope will reach you injoying the best of health & those few lines will inform you that I am yet on the land of the living & in very good health My Dear Love I recd a letter from you this Thursday which was adrested to Green Pond & it was written the 14th of Febry it was very old news though I was glad to do so & to read the sweet words that you wrote & oh how happy it made me to think you was praying to the mercyfully Father to Spare me through this cruel war & I am happy to say that I believe the Lord has heard our prayer for I have been in good health Ever since I have been in the Service, & I pray that I may remain so My Dear One I am now in the Sorryest country That I Ever saw we are right wher the Yankees has been near Except a few hogs & cows the Government gives us about half enough to eat I thought that we were fairing bad Enough at Green Pond but we were fairing well to what we are now My Dear One if you have and ten or twenty Dol bills you must get them changed for five Dols bills as all the ten & twentys is call in & you must do it right away you can get Mr Pfiaffer to take them I give you fives for them as I expect he will have a good many to return & I am happy to state to you that all is quiet hear no fighting going on & I hope this war will Soon End for I no that we will be a happy couple Dear I am hear cut out from a good many privileges though thank God I can yet raise my voice towards the heavens & the Lord will hear my prayer & let me Intreat you to continue in prayer for that is the Souls delight for I no not when I will get the chance to go home for it is impossible to get a furlow now but I hope we wont stay hear long but I hope the time will soon come when I may have the pleasure of kneeling down with you around the fireside as we so many times have done & their pray to the Almity Saivoir to help us in this world & prepare us to meet our dear Jesus at the right hand of glory & oh what a happy time that will be with us My Dear Sweet One give my love to the family it is no use to write to them for they wont write to me & kiss pretty little Corny for me & tell her that Brother Henry wants to see her very bad & all so write soon & direct your letter as I told you in my last one Though probbably you have not Recd it & for fear of that direct it thus H.G. Edenfield F Troop 5 Ga Cavl Lake City Florida My Dear Love as it is Impossible for me to get stamps I will send this without but I will send in this fifty cents of Ga money which is no use to me hear take good care of your Sweet Self Dear write me all the news & write Soon give my Respects to Thom Joyner & all the other Inquiring friends if any I am your esteemed One as Ever a friend & a husband till Death. I will write the other side to Annie

from Your husband Henry G. Edenfield

F. I Was Ordered to be Shot

The following account by Samuel J. Thorpe, (5th Georgia Cavalry, Liberty Independent Troop) who barely escaped execution by a firing squad, appeared in the March 16, 1901 edition of *The Atlanta Journal*. Around the turn of the century it became popular for southern newspapers to publish wartime letters and excerpts from those remaining veterans who had once worn gray.

The closest call I ever had during the memorable war between the states was after my capture by the Union forces, which occurred while vainly endeavoring to stop the advance of Sherman. The company I was a member of had been almost obliterated while engaged in driving Stoneman into the Chattahoochee river, which we finally accomplished, but not without terrible loss of life. Out of a company of 40 or 50 men only seven remained at the close of this struggle, including a lieutenant, a corporal and five privates. After a feeble resistance against General Sherman's forces near Augusta in the hasty retreat of our forces, the lieutenant, two privates and myself were captured and placed in a prison or stockade on the Ogeechee river, where we remained for several months, without a covering for our heads, and often when the northeast wind blew, stood for hours in water knee deep. From here we were moved to Hilton Head, S.C. where we lived on one pickle and a pint of meal each day until we again moved to some point in Virginia. It was about this time that some Union men who were foraging were captured and killed, and a few mutilated by southern men, who placed this warning on the foreheads of these men: "Death to all foragers."

Some Union generals, in retaliation for this act, ordered a number of Confederate prisoners, including myself, to be shot on a certain day. We were marched out and placed in position at about 7 in the morning. We were expecting at any time to hear the tread of the squad which was to send a volley into our helpless forms, and, sure enough, about 1 o'clock a squad came tramping in and stood about 20 yards in front of us and awaited the order to fire. The order never came, for a message was received from President Lincoln which saved us. The message was an order to return us to prison. Perhaps the message was inspired from the fact that many

Union prisoners would have suffered a like fate had our execution taken place as ordered.

Notes:

[1] Actually, there was considerable fighting around Brier Creek which is located near Waynesboro.

[2] Effingham county is located on the northwest corner of Chatham county and Savannah. Though Savannah was spared the torch, much of Effingham county burned. Today, it is difficult to find buildings in Effingham county that predate the war.

[3] Burke Davis in *Sherman's March* describes the action around Waynesboro, "Kilpatrick had camped on the railroad near the village of Waynesboro on November 26 when, about midnight, Wheeler's troopers galloped over them, scattering pickets, leaping log barricades and terrorizing the sleeping Federals. Wheeler took many prisoners, fifty horses, several regimental colors, and numerous blankets and over coats.... Fighting continued throughout the day of November 27 as Kilpatrick fell back from one barricade to another in some of the war's most furious cavalry clashes; galloping squadrons hurtled together with a ringing of sabers and crackling of pistols and carbines at point blank range.... Kilpatrick was saved by infantry hurried forward by General Slocum, a full division led by General Absalom Baird." See Davis, Burke. *Sherman's March*. New York: Random House, 1980., p.82.

[4] Despite continual naval bombardment by Union warships, Charleston remained in Confederate hands for the balance of the war. She was finally evacuated by Confederate forces on February 17, 1865 when her communication lines were severed by Sherman's men to the north. The garrison at Charleston, under the command of Gen. P.G.T. Beauregard, joined Gen. Johnston's forces in North Carolina for the battle of Bentonville.

[5] The Confederate government tried numerous times to meet with Lincoln to pursue peace, but Lincoln refused to give them an audience unless they were willing to rejoin the Union. Only once was there a meeting between the Davis administration and the Lincoln adminstration, but Lincoln did not attend and it was considered unofficial. Nothing concrete ever came from the meeting.

5

In a Yankee Prison Camp

Most students of the American Civil War are acquainted with Civil War prisons, particularly the infamous Andersonville prison in Georgia, as well as other southern prisons. Yet, many aren't familiar with northern prisoner of war camps. For example, Elmira, New York, was the sight of a Union prison camp nicknamed "Hellmira" for its hellish conditions. The horrors of this prison camp rivaled that of Andersonville. Tales of malnutrition, capturing and eating rats, scurvy, maggots, scant clothing, bitter weather, unsanitary conditions, disease, and death abound.

The southern populace as well as her soldiery were virtually starving by the end of the war, while the Union and her economy grew strong. The North had the means to care for the prisoners in her charge, therefore the question remains: Why did she allow southern prisoners of war to die of malnutrition, starvation, and sickness? Most agree that northern prisons were acting in retaliation against southern prisons.

Phoebe Yates Pember, a superintendent at Chimborazo Hospital in Richmond, penned the following words after witnessing a prisoner of war exchange: "Living and dead were taken from the flag-of-truce boat, not distinguishable save the difference of care exercised in moving them. The Federal prisoners we had released were in many instances in a like state, but our ports had been blockaded, our harvests burned, our cattle stolen, our country wasted.

Even had we felt the desire to succor, where could the wherewithal have been found? But the foe,—the ports of the world were open to him. He could have fed his prisoners upon milk and honey, and not have missed either."[1]

Needless to say, prisoner of war camps, North and South, were horrific places where men (guards—who were usually not combat soldiers, and prisoners) were thrown into an environment where this baser form of life brought out the demons of human nature. From the surgeon at Elmira who claimed to have killed more Rebels than any Union soldier to Salisbury prison in North Carolina where prisoners were packed together like sardines, men and boys of both the Blue and the Gray suffered depredations and hardships beyond description.[2]

B.W. Dorsey's narrative, though mild compared to other prison accounts, is one voice who seeks to describe such an experience, his experience at Camp Chase, Ohio.

Camp Chase was located on the outskirts of Columbus, Ohio. It was first used as a training camp for Union troops, but was soon converted into a prisoner of war camp. During the beginning of the war conditions in the camp were tolerable, but as men continued to pour in they gradually worsened. Shoddy barracks, open latrines, poor food, health problems and monotony soon became the norm. Joe Barbiere, a southern soldier imprisoned at Camp Chase early in the war, describes how prisoners became ill because of unsanitary conditions. He describes Camp Chase as being built on low flat ground, which was muddy, and how uncovered cisterns contaminated drinking water for a thousand prisoners, and sickness and dying soon followed.[3]

By the end of the war it is estimated that the Union army captured approximately 220,000 prisoners and that the Confederates captured more than 200,000 prisoners of war. 26,000 Confederates drew their last breath in prison camps, while 22,000 Federals died in southern prisons. Tragically, unlike any war before or since, both groups were Americans.

Dorsey's narrative does not contain the exact movements and military engagements of Lambright's narrative. Dorsey's account is more personal, more detailed, and deals with problems such as wondering where his next meal will come from or trying to find shoes for his horse. He gives us a glimpse into the every day life of a young cavalryman toward the end of the war and an account of life in a Civil War prison camp.

My how time flies! It has been 38 years since the close of our Civil War—The War Between The States—the most destructive war upon record, yet it is as fresh in my mind today as if it were last year.

During the four years of its continuance I had much experience. I belonged to Company D of the famous 5th Georgia Cavalry, which did service from Florida to Tennessee.

It was my misfortune to be captured by the enemy and held a prisoner of war for more than nine months, during which time I suffered much, and believing as I do, that a true story of my experience would be interesting to the older heads and profitable to the young and rising ones, I have concluded to give a brief sketch, hoping that my object will be accomplished and some good done.

In writing this brief narrative, it is not my purpose to speak of my soldier life more than to give the circumstances which led to my capture.

During the period of which I write, I kept notes, but in the lapse of time most of them have been mislaid, consequently I write partly from memory.

I will not deal in fiction, seasoned with rhetoric, but will give plain facts as they actually occurred, which will be verified to and endorsed by living witnesses.

B.W.D.

Some three weeks before Atlanta fell into the hands of the Federals, and while they were pressing Johns/t/on's army by flank movements by reason of their superior numbers, Gen. Johns/t/on offered Gen. Wheeler to take most of his efficient troops and move around in rear of Sherman's army and cut railroads, and burn his army supplies, hoping by this means to force him to fall back, or at least impede his progress, and thus peradventure save Atlanta.[4]

So on the 10th day of August, Wheeler concentrated his cavalry in and near Covington, and hastily ordered his subordinate officers to select the best mounted men from their respective commands and prepare for a raid in rear of the Yankee army.

Owning to heavy duty the last several weeks in suppressing raids of the enemy—many times making a forced march twenty or more miles in the severe heat without stopping to rest or feed, as a natural and reasonable consequence, many horses were adjudged / judged/ too badly worn and jaded to make a raid inside the enemy's lines to such an extent as were contemplated.

In fact, many had already been sent to the recruiting camp.

I belonged to Company D of the famous 5th Georgia. This had been a large regiment numbering over 1,000 well mounted men but as some had been killed, some wounded, horses had been killed and some run down, so only about half of our regiment were selected and put in line for raid.

Only one commissioned officer of my company was in line: Lieut. John E. Zonks, a noble and brave soldier.

My captain, William Hughes, had his horse killed in that memorable charge our regiment made upon the Yankees at Noon Day Church, led by the 2nd Squadron (companies D and I) some two before, and had never reached his command again. I never saw him again during the war.

Gen. Anderson had been wounded, and Col. Roberson was brevetted to command our brigade. Gen. Kelly was in command of the division.

So about dark that evening, about 600 well mounted cavalrymen took up the line of march with a yell from one end of the column to the other, which made the welkin /?/ ring, and which seemed to infuse new life into the whole command.

It is not for me or any other private soldier to know just where or what point we were to strike, but suffice it to say we made a circuitous route around the left wing of the Federal army—moving very cautiously.

The night was clear, but no moonlight. We marched all night, and at nightlight our brigade halted to rest and feed. Other commands had taken other roads for the purpose, I suppose, to find feed for horses.

We were soon in our saddles again, and that evening a little after nightfall we entered Dalton.

Some of our troops had already taken possession of the place and were feasting upon Yankee army Supplies. The little garrison was taking refuge in the stockade and remained there all night unmolested by our men.

After resting a while and feeding horses on oats, which we found in the commissary, we went to work tearing up the railroad tracks.

Tearing up a railroad is no easy job for a fellow inexperienced in the business. We worked nearly all night, and next morning we mounted our steeds and left town.

The garrison of Federals opened fire upon us and our regiment was selected to cover the retreat.

We dismounted, "linked horses,"[5] and returned the fire and held them in check, falling back as occasion required, and after a hot skirmish, we mounted horses, and to our great sorrow and mortification it was learned that L.S. Lanier of my company, a noble boy, had been killed and left in the hands of the enemy: also Lieut. Conror of Company F was wounded, but was brought up and taken to a house and left in care of a citizen.

We marched on to Spring Place and there rested one day and night.

Pickets were thrown out around the camp as a matter of course. I was detailed with one squad and stationed near a house in which a family lived, and our instructions were to allow no communication with the family by their neighbors, by not allowing anyone to leave or enter the premises during our stay.

This precaution was taken because we were inside the enemy's lines, and to avoid betrayal into their hands—not knowing who was friend or who was foe.

Soon after we were posted we saw two ladies coming walking down the road towards the house. The sentinel on post expressed a delicacy in challenging a lady. I volunteered to take his place; so taking his gun I met the ladies and challenged them, and explained to them our orders.

I suppose every picket had the same orders, and if they were faithful in obeying them, these two ladies certainly had to lie out in the woods that night.

Leaving Spring Place, we crossed over into Tennessee and crossed the Hinachie River.

In this section we encountered many bushwhackers.[6] They were composed of deserters from the Confederate armies and citizens who were disloyal to the confederate cause. As they would fire upon us from ambush, our advance guard would deploy and scour the woods until they succeeded in capturing them, except in a few cases they escaped to the mountains. When captured, they were either shot or hanged to a limb on a tree.

We camped one night about nine miles from Athens, having nothing to eat for men or horse except green apples and green corn, an abundance which grew in that section.

Next day we passed through Athens and halted awhile, during which time some of our men were tearing up the railroad.

In Athens, as in many places, some of the ladies demonstrated their loyalty to the Confederate cause by waving their handkerchiefs and their private Confederate flags.

I could but say in my heart, God bless the women of the South! But here and there the Union flag was waving as if in proud defiance.

Here in East Tennessee was a light sprinkling of people who seemed to be opposed to the Confederate cause.

One day while on advance guard with instructions to have some bread cooked at Sweet Water, a small village on the Knoxville road, one of the ladies to whom we applied readily agreed and went at it with a vim, but soon gave us to understand that she was no friend to us.

It fell to my lot to do the talking and I discovered that she, like most of the common class of East Tennessee, in talking used the adjunct "uns" to pronouns. So our talk ran into the following:

She said, "Weunns whipped some of youuns the other day down in Georgia."

"No, mam," said I. "Weuns always whip youuns only when youuns plank us by over balance in numbers."

I asked her to what point she referred.

"At Decatur weuns whipped youuns bad."

I assured her that she was mistaken, for there had been no fight there except a small raiding part of Yanks entered the place and my command got after them, and the Yanks ran, so we couldn't get a fight.

She fully believed they had whipped us for it was in the papers, she said.

I asked her for the paper containing the news. She gave it to me and I found that it was "in the papers" sure enough.

I proved to her by my companions that we were actually in the engagement referred to and that the statement was false.

From the paper, we learned that Knoxville was held by a strong force and well fortified, whither we were tending.

The command marched on until nearly daylight the next morning, then resting a few hours and crossed the Tennessee River, surrounded Knoxville and on coming near Strawbury /Strawberry/ Plains it was ascertained that the enemy held the place with some force, but it seemed that our officers intended giving them a fight.

So "linking horses," we dismounted, formed line of battle and marched up the hill near the town. A few shots were fired from the skirmish line, but as dark came on, no other advance was made.

We lay in line of battle all night suffering intense hunger—not for Yankee blood particularly, but for something that would satisfy the inner man, as we had nothing to eat for nearly two days except green apples.

A pleasing incident occurred during the night, but I must pass on with my story.

Next morning, it was decided not to attack the place, so we mounted our horses and turned our course towards the Cumberland Mountains. That day we halted a little before night and struck camp for the night in order to secure feed for men and horses.

I was one that foraged for horse feed while others butchered some mutton and obtained flour from a mill near by.

My squad had some difficulty in finding forage, but finally we found a lot of wheat shocked in a field about two miles from camp. Without asking permission of any one, we loaded our horses.

No one but a cavalryman knows how much he can tie to his saddle. It is no job to carry seventy or eighty pounds of wheats or oats in the straw.

It was after dark when we reached the camp; it being dark and the locality strange to us, it was with some difficulty that we found our original commands.

But we reached our regimental line all right, and my organs of smell told me that supper was being cooked, and on nearing the fire, I found that our company's cook had roasted a lot of mutton and baked a pile of "slap jacks" about knee high.

My hunger rose to its highest pitch as I had eaten nothing but green apples for the last three days and insisted that our cook make haste for I was hungry, tired and sleepy.

His reply to me was not satisfactory which elicited from me some uncomplimentary words.

It was dropped however, and in a few moments he announced "all ready," and right then and there we ate one of the best meals of our lives; or at least enjoyed it best.

After leaving camp next morning, nothing of special interest occurred, except many of our horses began to show signs of lameness from having lost one or more shoes.

In this rocky country, a horse soon becomes lame if he travels much without shoes.

My horse lost one off his hind foot before we left Georgia, but having a hard hoof, he traveled all right so far.

This caused much uneasiness as we were in the territory of the enemy. But our officers gave us permission to exchange with any citizen if we so desired.

Good horses were scarce in that section at that time as the Yankees had already pressed the best of them.

We reached the foot of the Cumberland Mountain just below the Gap and ascended that afternoon and camped on the mountain, and next morning we resumed our march.

The road was plain and showed much travel. The water spouts which issued from these perpendicular walls of rock along the road side were perfectly magnificent and refreshing to a weary and thirsty soldier.

The weather was excessively hot, men and horses were jaded.

About the middle of that afternoon we reached the foot of the mountain, which put us in what was called Middle Tennessee.

Here we struck a thickly settled community of people of culture and refinement, and some of the richest lands I ever saw.

These people showed many acts of kindness to us, manifesting true loyalty /loyalty/ to the Confederate cause.

Our command rested for the night and made arrangements to have horses shod—there being several blacksmith shops in the community.

Next day the troops all moved on towards Murfreesboro except about one hundred or more of us whose horses needed shoes, and Col. Dibril /Dibrell/, who commanded a regiment of our brigade, and a few of his men whose homes were in Middle Tennessee.

Dibril and his men were permitted to visit their homes for a couple of days and meet /met/ us at Lebanon at a certain hour of the second day, where he was to take command of us and lead us to the remainder of our brigade.

Captain Bradsford of the 5th Georgia was left in command of the squad. Our time expired all our horses were shod and had to leave in order to meet Col. Dibril at Lebanon at the appointed time.

I was one who failed to get my horse shod, but after two days rest he showed but little sign of lameness, and I entertained hope of his making the trip until I could either get him shod or exchange him for another as some others had done, but as he was a good one, I intended holding on to him as long as he was able to travel well.

While on our way to Lebanon to meet Col. Dibrel and his men, we were permitted to march at leisure, and at times we were considerably scattered.

There were no Federal soldiers in that immediate section and we felt comparatively secure though we were few in number.

While riding along, I noticed a road leading off to a plantation a few hundred yards from the turnpike which we were traveling.

Just as I conceived an idea that by going in that place I could obtain a fresh horse; so without telling the boys my object, I took the road and in a few minutes was at the gate.

A middle aged lady and her little daughter came out of the gate and spoke to me. She recognized me as Confederate by my dress.

I at once told her to what command I belonged and my business of motive in coming by.

She told me that her husband was in the Confederate army, and the Yankees had taken every horse from her, and robbed her of many things. She expressed her regret at not being able to furnish me with a fresh horse. She talked so kindly and interestingly that I delayed some time.

As I was about to take my leave, she asked if I would have something to eat. I thanked her in the affirmative.

She hastily brought me a dish of cold chicken pie, a plat of biscuits and a pitcher of milk; telling me at the same time that she could not invite me into her home as the Yanks had forbidden her from entertaining the Rebs, and she wanted a clear conscience in telling them she had not.

I commended her for this, and at the same time I seated myself upon a large rock which lay near the gate.

I hastily ate my unexpected meal, and while eating I heard her tell her daughter to go in the house and look in a certain place and get a pair of socks and bring them to her.

The girl obeyed her mother and in a few moments the good lady gave them to me—a pair of home knit wool socks; and at the same time told me to take the remainder of the biscuits for future use, which I did.

Putting the bread and socks in my haversack, I asked her name and she told me her name was Smith.

I then expressed to her my gratitude, assuring her that Providence would reward her some day.

I now realized I was far behind my comrades, and mounting my horse, I struck a gallop to overtake them.

I road only a few hundred yards before I met a colored man as he came in by a road driving two fine mules to a wagon.

I halted him and demanded a change. I told him that my horse was a little lame, and that I had orders to force an exchange for any horse or mule that I found fit for service. He readily submitted as I assured him that my horse would work in the wagon.

Without further preliminary, I hastily threw my saddle upon the mule and mounted.

As I looked down the road beside me, I saw at a distance several horsemen coming whom I took to be Yankees; but later on I found they were some of my own command who, like myself had been straggling.

But thinking they were Yankees and that I was in danger of falling into their hands, I put spurs to my mule which proved to be a great traveler, and in almost no time I was in Lebanon where the command had stopped to await the arrival of Col. Dibril and his men.

Several of our men had exchanged for mules, but mine seemed to be the finest looking, and I was vain enough to boast of my good luck.

I at once inquired for my friend Sam Zoucks and gave him some of my biscuit which my good lady friend had given me.

I did this because he and I had agreed to devide /sic/ with each other any eatables which either of us was fortunate enough to secure by foraging.

An hour or so later, Captain Brailsford came to me, accompanied by a gentleman in citizen's dress, riding a fine horse and leading mine, and introduced him to me as Mr. Green; Captain Brailsford explained to me that Mr. Green was the owner of the mule I had taken from the negro and that Mr. Green desired me to exchange back.

I reminded him of the order given us to press into service horses or mules which we found suitable for service, and that while my horse was a good one, he was liable to fall and I be left.

Mr. Green remonstrated with me, saying that he was a good Southerner, and that he had already given fourteen head of horses to the Confederate army.

I then turned to him and addressed him in the following language: "Well, Mr. Green, doubtless you are all right, and I don't doubt your statement or loyalty, but while you have given fourteen horses to the Confederate service, and doubtless many other things, yet you haven't given as much as I have, for I have given my only horse and myself, too, and I see that you still have three head left, and yourself not in service either."

This made the boys laugh, and I felt like I was master of the situation. But Captain Brailsford took me off to one side and talked to me and advised me to exchange back with Mr. Green, and that I could soon get another. This he did persuasively and not imperatively.

As I liked the captain so well and had confidence in his judgement /sic/, I consented to exchange, and Mr. Green went off on his way rejoicing.

After waiting at Lebanon a few hours, Col. Dibril and his men came together with some twenty or thirty recruits well mounted but with no arms, except a few of them had shotguns. This swelled our squad to 150 or 200 men.

Among the recruits was a man of about fifty years of age, of medium height, but would weigh at least 250 pounds whose name was Govall.

He was a very profane man and swore vengeance against the Yankees for the many wrongs they had done him and his neighbors; and by joining the army he hoped to be able to wreck vengeance upon some of them, at least.

I will find it necessary to use this gentleman's name several times in the sequel of this narrative.

Col. Dibril took command, formed us in line that afternoon and marched in the direction of Mufreesboro.

Just before night we halted, fed horses and butchered a beef; but as we had no time to cook, each fellow took a piece of raw beef and put it in his haversack.

As I was especially fond of beef liver, I put a piece in my haversack, hoping soon to have time to broil it and have one more good meal of beef liver with the remainder of the biscuit which I still had in my haversack.

But about that time a courier conveyed a dispatch to Col. Dibril that our main raiding force had engaged a force of Yankees between Murfreesboro and Nashville, and that Gen. Kelly, our division commander had been killed; and for him (Col. Dibril) to hasten to their relief without delay.

The colonel determined at once, if possible, to lead us to our command that night. As he was acquainted with the roads, he took a circuitous route, and through the darkness of night we rode rapidly until after midnight when he halted to rest and feed horses.

I saw no hope of getting a fresh horse, but by some inspiration my horse seemed all right.

There being a field of corn near by we hastily fed our horses. But about the time I got my horse fed, and was in the act of lying down upon the ground to rest, I was detailed to go out on picket post with Robert and Taylor Walthour of my regiment and Abbot of the 8th Alabama.

We were posted near by a large residence situated on a big road about four or five hundred yards west of our camp.

Abbot and I took the first watch while the Walthours slept. Abbot watched in one direction while I watched the other, which led in the direction of the residence.

I soon dismounted, tied my horse and walked cautiously up in front of the house to see if I could see or hear any one about the premises.

While there I saw a dim light in a negro house a short distance up the lane. I cautiously approached the house and gently knocked at the door.

The occupants seemed to be asleep but soon awoke, and I soon found that some woman and children occupied the house.

I asked if they had seen any rebels about there recently, feigning myself to be a Federal soldier.

To this they replied negatively, but they had heard that some of them had been around Murfreesboro and had played havoc with the railroad and were fighting the Yankees in the direction of Nashville.

I then went back, mounted my horse and remained on post until our time expired when the Walthours boys relieved us.

I dismounted, and being so anxious to sleep, I took no time to take my rubber and blanket from my saddle, but lay down upon the ground, holding my bridle reins in my hand, and in almost no time was sound asleep.

In a seemingly short time I was suddenly awakened by a rumbling noise as if a mighty raging storm or an earthquake like unto that which destroyed ancient Lisbon.

I sprang to my feet and saw it was day dawn and Bob Walthour cried out, "Yankees, boys!"

I looked and through an open wood, southward I saw a column of Yankee cavalry charging our camp at full speed, yelling as soldiers do on like occasions.

Photo Gallery

SCOUTS OUT: **The 5th Georgia Cavalry, by Greg Seamands.**

Confederate Monument, Liberty County Georgia, notice the cavalry boots, hat, and sabre, *photograph by author.*

Fort Thunderbolt, Savannah, from *Harper's Pictorial History of the Civil War.*

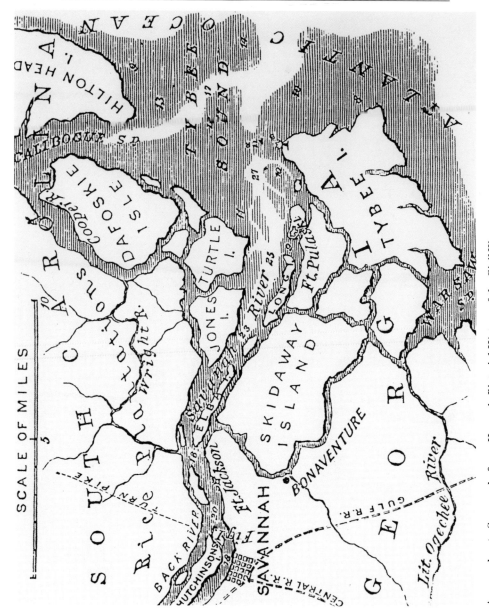

Approaches to Savannah, from *Harper's Pictorial History of the Civil War.*

U.S. Customs House (built 1852) in Savannah. Sherman stood on the roof to gaze out over the city he had conquered without firing a shot, *photograph by author.*

Former home of the British Consul at Savannah, Edmund Molyneux. The home was later used as headquarters and residence by Union General Oliver O. Howard and his successor, General William F. Barry, during the occupation of Savannah. Some sources state that after their departure over $10,000 worth of furnishings had been damaged or confiscated, much of the wine cellar ransacked, and many books from the library stolen. In 1885 the house was puchased by former Confederate General Henry Jackson; he lived there until his death in 1898. The house is now occupied by a private club. *photograph by author.*

Green-Meldrim House where Sherman stayed while in Savannah, *photograph by author.*

General Sherman reviewing his army on Bay Street in Savannah, January 1865, drawing by William Waud, *courtesy Library of Congress.*

Confederate Raiders, from *Harper's Pictorial History of the Civil War.*

General Joseph Wheeler, C.S.A., *photograph from author's collection.*

General William Tecumseh Sherman, U.S.A., *courtesy Library of Congress.*

General Joseph Johnston, C.S.A., *photograph from author's collection.*

Federal soldiers in captured fort, Atlanta, *courtesy Library of Congress.*

Small arms surrendered by Johnston's army, from *Harper's Pictorial History of the Civil War.*

Impromptu Barricade, from *Harper's Pictorial History of the Civil War*.

Confederate Prisoners being conducted from Jonesboro to Atlanta, from *Harper's Pictorial History of the Civil War.*

Skirmishing in the woods near Atlanta, from *Harper's Pictorial History of the Civil War.*

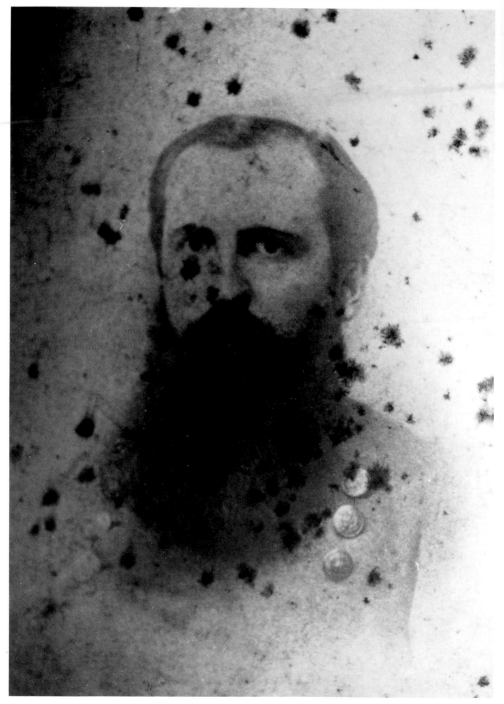

Brigadier General Robert H. Anderson, 5th Georgia Cavalry, *courtesy Georgia Historical Society.*

David H. Porter, Chaplain 5th Georgia Cavalry, *courtesy First Presbyterian Church, Savannah.*

Confederate POWs, Camp Chase, Ohio, *courtesy Library of Congress.*

Robert William DeLoach, 5th Georgia Cavalry. After the war Robert and brother Z. Taylor DeLoach built DeLoach's mill and constructed dams for people who wanted ponds. Robert went on to serve in the state legislature and died on March 4, 1930, at the age of eighty-seven, *courtesy of Special Collections, Henderson Library, Georgia Southern University.*

Ruins of Old Sheldon Church, South Carolina. Though Savannah was spared the torch, Federal troops quickly resumed their destruction soon after they crossed into South Carolina. Sheldon Church had been burned by British troops 86 years earlier, rebuilt in 1826, only to be razed once more. It wasn't rebuilt again, *photograph by author.*

Historical marker, Old Sheldon Church, *photograph by author.*

The interior walls of the church, still charred from the flames, *photograph by author.*

Sherman's army entering Resaca, from *Harper's Pictorial History of the Civil War.*

Destruction of General Hood's ordnance train, Atlanta, *courtesy Library of Congress.*

Augustus Lewis Cowart, 5th Georgia Cavalry, Co. E, *courtesy Georgia Department of Archives and History.*

Corporal John Leary, Liberty Independent Troop, Co. G, 5th Georgia Cavalry, *courtesy, "U.S. Army Photograph," Ft. Stewart, GA.*

Some of the members of Philadelphia Lodge No. 73, F & AM. This photo was made in 1889 in front of the lodge building used at that time. Shown, left to right, G. Godwin, J. J. Barnard, A. F. DeLoach, Edward Weathers, Aquilla Weathers, Miles Dubberly, William Dubberly, J. J. DeLoach, Jonathan Barnard, Asa Barnard, Jack DeLoach, Glenn Thompson, Joe P. Collins, F. D. Griffin and A. H. Prince. It will be of interest that Glennville was named in 1889 for Glenn Thompson, a local school teacher, shown fourth from the right. Prior to that Glennville was known as Philadelphia. The post office was established here at that time. Veterans of the 5th Georgia Cavalry include: Jonathan Barnard, Edward Weathers, and Aquilla Weathers. *Courtesy Ann DeLoach, Claxton, GA.*

Confederates dragging guns up Kennesaw mountain. The Union, frustrated by flanking movements, decided on a frontal assault against heavily fortified Confederate positions. Wave after wave of brave men in blue fell before a withering fire of musketry and artillery. In a few hours the Union offensive lay in a crumpled heap. The Federals suffered over 3,000 casualties. Confederate losses were estimated at about 750. *drawing by A.R. Waud, from Battles and Leaders.*

The Atlanta Campaign was costly for both Confederate and Union armies. Men from the ranks up to major generals were killed in action. This sketch shows Confederate General Leonidas Polk being mortally wounded by an artillery shell while he, General Hardee, and General Joseph Johnston (center) were reconnoitering Union positions from the summit of Pine Mountain on the morning of June 14, 1864. *drawing courtesy of Library of Congress.*

Another view of Camp Chase. These buildings were initially used as barracks for new recruits before the camp was converted into a prison. *courtesy National Archives.*

Abbot and I instantly sprang into our saddles and went at full speed for our camp.

The Walthour boys being already mounted on post had the advantage of us in getting the start and succeeded in reaching camp before the charging Yankees did.

My friend Abbot and I saw we could not reach camp before the enemy, and that it would be foolish as well as perilous to rush into camp at that instant as it was evident they were stampeded; and we well knew they were not prepared to make a successful fight.

So we reined up our horses and turned our course down a steep to our left a hundred or more yards.

In this ravine or gully we encountered a stream of water which seemed to be impassible /sic/ since which time some called it "Duck River."

We dismounted, left our horse and ran further down the steep near the waters edge and concealed ourselves behind a huge rock.

Occasionally we could see a squad of Yankees across the ravine scouring the woods as if in search of Rebs whom they suspected as being hid.

Our condition was evidently a critical one, and what was best to do was a question hard to decide. It was certain that our men had been stampeded and many captured and perhaps some killed.

We hastily consulted as to what to do. "A thousand thoughts revolved" in my mind.

To reach our command seemed impossible; in fact we did not know but what the command had been annihilated, and being several hundred miles inside the enemy's line, and a strange part of the country to us, and the enemy in arms at almost every cross road, I could see no way or hope of reaching home or our main command even if we escaped that crowd; and in all probability we would be captured and condemned as spies.

I was in favor of surrendering and risk our fate with them. Abbot would say nothing, but left it all with me.

We remained there in terrible suspense from daylight until the sun was far up above the tree tops when we saw two blue coats ride up to our horses, one dismounting to take the bridles.

We at once rose and gave the signal of surrender: they reciprocated and we advanced, leaving our carbines.

I forgot my pistol which was belted to my person, and when they discovered it they came near shooting me for not disarming myself, but I hastily unbuckled and gave it to them.

They talked very kindly to us and told us they had captured several of our men, but most of them had escaped through towards Woodbury.

They allowed us to ride our horses and they took us to town (Murfreesboro) whither they had carried the other prisoners, a distance of about two miles.

We learned that it was the 9th Pennsylvania Cavalry that made the charge that morning, having learned our whereabouts by means of scouts, but I am persuaded to believe that some citizens betrayed us into their hands for a little booty.

As we neared the town, we came up with other prisoners where they were waiting in line—about 75 or so in number, among whom were several of the 5th Georgia and my own company who greeted us with laughter, and asked me where I had been.

I had no time to explain, but joined them in the laugh. "Misery loves company," it is said, and I have seen it verified more than once.

After dismounting and falling in line and all horses led off, I discovered that almost every prisoner had taken his blanket and haversack, but I had forgotten to take mine as they were tied to my saddle, and oh, how I hated to lose my haversack containing my socks and beef liver which I had procured the day before! Especially did I hate to lose my rubber[7] which I had picked up on the battle field of Olustee, Florida.

We were marched to an open shed or lumber house and put under guard of some infantry. Our men having cut the railroad so badly north of Murfreesboro, we could not be conveyed to prison for about six days.

We soon understood that we were to be sent to Camp Chase, Ohio, and there held as prisoners of war.

In making out the role of prisoners the following were the names of the 5th Georgia: Capt. Wm. Brailsford, Lieut. J.E. Zoucks, T.I. Grice, S.H. Zoucks, T.F. Linder, F. Williams, J.S. Kicklighter, Math

Miller, W.P. Merritt, D.R. McIntosh, W.H. Thompson, F. Roe, D.H. Bailey, W. Maney, E.J. Zeigler, P.W. Wells, and myself.

Just hear I will state that Heary /Harry/ Kicklighter and Charles Baker of our regiment were captured some days later and conveyed to the same prison with us.

We remained six days in Mufreesboro. While there we were fed slightly on hard tack and old ned (bacon). Some of the old citizens came to see us and talked kindly; also a Miss Walker, a female physician, who had been a surgeon in Sherman's army and who had been captured by our men and exchanged.

She talked very freely and intelligently—seemed to be posted as to the movements of contending armies, but now and then would make some sarcastic flings at the South, Captain Brailsford with his ready wit, would "down" her occasionally to the great amusement of the prisoners.

One of the gentlemen who accompanied her to our quarters remarked to me that it was a shame for soldiers to capture and imprison a refined lady like Miss Walker.

In reply to this I told him that if a "refined lady" like Miss Walker put herself in a position of that kind she should suffer the consequences.

While there, I suffered much with cold. We had been out on the raid six weeks, my clothing thin and badly worn, the September winds spreading their way through that open shed, all combined made me feel very uncomfortable.

The railroad repaired, we marched to the depot to take our departure for Camp Chase, Ohio.

While there waiting for the train, one of the guards and I got into a jangle. I recognized a prisoner's right—a right to talk.

I told him that I was on Southern soil and if I had my way, I would exterminate every Yankee south of the Mason Dixon line.

He called me a Johnie Reb (a name they gave to all of Johns/t/on's army) and I called him a blue bellied Yankee.

He denied being a Yankee, and said that he was as much a southerner as I was.

I asked him from what state he was. He said he was from Tennessee. I then told him that I now thought less of him than ever before; for a man who would rebel against his native state and join an invading host and assist in laying waste her beauty and grandeur was a traitor of the deepest dye.

The prisoners laughed and cheered—some one shouting out, "Ho-ra for Dixie!"

The officer of the guard restored quiet and we were soon on our way to Camp Chase, Ohio.

About night, the train rolled into Nashville where we remained all night locked up in the yard of the prison.

Next morning we were formed in line and each fellow received a piece of fat bacon and a slice of light bread from the hands of a surly black negro.

We were soon on our way again, and at Louisville, Kentucky, we were put under guard of another set of soldiers—calling us all kind of abusive names. We learned that they belonged to the 45th New York Regiment.

Tom Grice asked them if they had ever been to the front. They said they had not. He told them he well knew they had not without asking the question; that if they had been to the front they would have found much harder job to catch a fellow than it was to exult over him after he was caught by some one else, and if they didn't believe it, just go and try it—that he had always found that those who lie around easy places, such as guard houses and hospitals were the ones to do the boasting and crowing over prisoners.

This he said with considerable emphasis which somewhat quieted the fellows.

We arrived at the city of Columbus after dark and were at once conducted to the prison which was about a mile from the city.

The night was dark and the wind boisterous and cool, but as we were marched at quick step we were very warm by the time we reached our destination.

I couldn't see the outside surroundings, but we were required to pass through a kind of office and each gave the number of his regiment and letter of his company.

We were all searched, taking away all knives and greenbacks if any chanced to have a little.

I had a Confederate bill, but as they had no use for it, I was allowed to keep my money.

They gave a blanket to each one who had none, then opened a large gate and turned us in prison number 2.

It being after "taps," everything was still as death save the sentinels who walked their beats upon the parapets. A guard conducted us to quarters, most of us going to Barracks Number 8.

That was a miserable night to me. I was cold, hungry, sleepy and tired.

The barracks seemed to be full of other prisoners, but having no light we couldn't see them, and being night we were not allowed to talk above a whisper.

In the course of time, daylight came and we could see our surroundings.

The prison covered four or five acres of ground, enclosed by a plank wall some twelve feet high, with two partitions, forming three separate prisons.

There were barracks erected in which to sleep. These houses were about 100 feet long by 20 feet wide with a door in one end, with three rows of shelves or bunks on either side, affording each barracks a capacity of holding about 200 men.

I had had nothing to eat for two days and was truly glad to learn that was the day for issuing rations, so sometime that day we drew two days' rations which consisted of eight hard tacks and a piece of mackerel about the size of my hand for each one of us.

I could have eaten it all at once, but knowing that I was to get no more for two days, I ate very little and carefully wrapped it up and put it on my bunk, under my blanket.

That night I went for it—and behold it was gone! Some rogue had stolen it.

For me to stand another two days, it seemed more than I could bear.

My two bunk mates, Tom Grice and Sam Zonks, however, cheerfully divided with me, so with much suffering I survived another two days, when we drew the same amount for another two days.

The fish we drew were very salty and called for a free use of water of which I drank freely. I became very sick and set to vomiting, and for several hours I was as sick a fellow as ever lived. I never see mackeral /sic/ now but think of that day.

I soon got well, however; and retained my health the balance of my prison life.

The prisoners were not confined to the barracks, but were allowed to walk about inside the prison so as not to cross what was called the "dead line" which was in about ten feet of the wall or parapet on the top of which the sentry walked.

There were men there from every state in the Confederacy; also some few from other states who were imprisoned for expressing sympathy for the South.

Men of every class of character were there.

As to suffering, no human speech could express my feelings at times. The weather in that latitude was intensely cold for a South Georgian, especially for one with no clothing except a ragged summer suit of grey.

We had plenty of soap and water, but food and fire were scarce articles; in fact we had no fire except at a little wash house where we were allowed a little fire to boil and wash our clothes, but the scanty allowance of wood was green and the fire refused to burn freely, consequently we found it a hard job to wash only in cold water.

We had no garments to wear while we tried to wash the dirt and dust out of our well worn suits.

I tried to wash a few times but finally gave it up as a bad job and hired a fellow prisoner to wash for me—giving him a part of my scanty rations. Many others did the same thing.

"Every man to his calling." But I decided that I was not called to wash clothes. It is certain that our clothes were washed but seldom.

The bunks for sleeping were just wide enough for two men but three of us agreed to bunch and squeeze in together; so we lay in one blanket and covered with two.

I lay in the middle through choice. All three lay on one side, and when one turned over all three had to turn at the same time.

I slept very little but would lie there and shiver with cold, listening to the wailing of the wind as it sped around the building giving us an occasional puff through the cracks.

At daylight reveille was sounded and we were required to be in line to roll call outside the barracks.

The sergeant of the prison who came every morning to call the roll was named Plum, and a close fellow he was, but he seemed to care little how long he kept us out in the wind and snow for he was well wrapped in his overcoat.

Aside from cold and hunger, I suffered a great deal mentally. The idea of being confined to the limits of the prison—shut out from the world—not knowing when, if ever, I could get out of that miserable place, when could I hear from home or they hear what had become of me?

But we were informed that there had been an arrangement between the two governments for prisoners to write to their homes, and letters conveyed across lines by flags of truce.

But as a matter of course these letters would be examined by the authorities before leaving.

So Sam Zonks and I at once procured paper (the Yankees furnished the material) and wrote to our fathers, enclosing both in the same envelope, directing it to Ilinesville, our country site.

In about three weeks time I was informed that there was a letter for me at the "Gate."

So I hastened to the gate, and gave my name, command to which I belonged and number of barracks I occupied.

The letter being directed accordingly it was given me and I at once recognized the handwriting as that of my father.

Never before had I received a letter that gave me as much joy. He merely stated that he had received my note and that the Federals had reached and captured Savannah /December 20, 1864/ and that some of their cavalry were camping near his house and they were kind etc.

Of course he could write nothing disparagingly of them for his letter like mine had been examined before it was sent.

Some time during the month of December there was a stove put in each barracks which proved some help in decreasing the suffering from the cold.[8]

But for 100 to 200 men to one stove, it was rather "crowding the monkey." And the house was so open it could retain no heat scarcely.

Once in a while someone whose home was inside the Federal lines would receive a little box of eatables from their homes which would supplement their scant rations for a few days.

While this was allowed, they were not allowed to receive anything like clothing.[9]

I learned there that a lady of Tennessee sent her son an overcoat and he was refused to receive it.

Many are in torment today wailing, weeping and g/n/ashing their teeth for their treatment to prisoners during that eventful period.

Almost every disease known to man prevailed in that prison. Smallpox was a specialty. This disease raged most furiously during the coldest weather.

We were all vaccinated. It took well with me and I was right sick a day or two and I thought I was a "goner," but kind providence permitted me to escape for which I am very greatful /*sic*/.

But two of my company, Fred Williams and T.F. Linder succum/b/ed to this disease while there.[10]

They were two as good men as belonged to our regiment— good Christian men as well as good soldiers.

I shall never forget some of the good counsel Uncle Fred gave me while in the army. (We all called him uncle as he was our senior.)

Neither will I forget the warm handshake he gave me when he told me good bye on leaving for the pest house while the smallpox was very visible upon his face.

There were more men died in prison than died in the army in proportion to number.

At least 30 or 40 dead were carried out of prison some days from various diseases.

There was a man sick in my barracks suffering pneumonia. One morning when we arose for roll call, this man was found by the stove dead.

He had crawled from his bunk in his agony of suffering and died while trying to get warm.

I have already said that I suffered much mentally. Yes, I did. I longed for the sight of a hog or horse or dog or any thing besides those miserable men.

I was always fond of reading, but nothing to read to while away the weary hours—not even an almanac.

How I wished for my Testament my sister gave me when I bade her good bye the last time! But I left it in my saddle bags when I left the Georgia front thinking of being back in a few days.

One day a young man about my age, a Marylander, received a little box from his home in Baltimore in which were a few Bibles for free distribution among the prisoners.

He gave me one and I read it over and over again. I have that Bible yet, on the fly leaf of which was written with pencil my name and the number of my mess, barracks, and prison.

It was my nature to want to walk, and move about and when I could walk the place over and over which was a relief to my mind as well as good for my health.

Much of the time it was too wet to walk around, so I was confined to my barracks most of the day time as well as all the night.

As I lay on my cold hard bunk, my mind was upon the past. I thought of my school days —how I use to play with Jim, Joe, Oss, Berry, Mack and the negro boys with whom I had played and coon hunted, and ate as much as we wanted and made big fires and warmed as much as wanted to.

There was Jim, Sandy, Munn, Jack and Len. These were the happy days but we didn't realize it then.

I thought of my father's table heavily loaded with the substantials of life—where there was plenty to spare.

I thought that I could never leave a table again without eating all that was on it.

As I thought and dreamed of these things a gnawling /gnawing/ sensation would lay hold on me and I would often involuntarily rise to a sitting posture.

My mind also ran back to the big dinner I used to enjoy at the Fourth of July celebrations, and the May day Sunday school dinners, and the places if feasting, and I could never lie or sit still.

Especially did my mind run back to the day when my company left home for the army and the young ladies flattered us with their bequests, when, in a responsive speech I pledged my loyalty to their interest and to the Confederate cause.

I surveyed the three long years of my soldier life, and could call to mind no act of mine of which I was ashamed: I had kept my vow and my conscience was clear.

In this place, I learned to sympathize with anything I knew to be hungry or cold.

I never let my horses go hungry, and if I get so I cannot feed them plentifully I will sell out and have none. If my hogs squeal out after me for something to eat I scarcely fail to give them some thing.

If my children get hungry, I want them to eat plentifully for I know what hunger is in the full sense of the word.

I had been a wild, reckless boy, but there I promised the good Lord that if I were spared I would live a better life, which vow I have endeavored to keep until this hour.

There were men there of all classes and character. There were some who possessed good principles and refinement, showing that they had been well raised, but most of them had descended the scale of moral degradation so low till they had lost all self respect, or respect for any one else.

Though a boy, I learned a good deal of human nature. Men are corrupt, and when exposed to evils incident to camp and prison life for four years one gets quite low in the scale of moral life unless his early training had been good or in possession of genuine religion.

I saw men playing cards and swearing the most profane oaths ever issued from human lips, within arms reach of dead and dying men. Yes, gambling for each others rations and clothing.

Men would steal from each other and fight for the most frivolous cause.

One night, soon after entering the place, some fellow stole my blanket off my bunk and my bunk mates and I were forced to make out with two blankets until I found a chance to buy one for a day's rations from a fellow who had more than he had use for.

It may be that I bought my own blanket though I could not tell as there were a hundred or more just alike in our barracks.

The devil was there doing his mighty work. The U.S. government got away with the devil however, when it excluded whiskey and fiddles from the Yankee prisons, for they are his most successful instruments.

If the sergeant of the prison was informed of any misdemeanor and the guilty one found, he would have him punished in a peculiar and novel way.

If he were convicted for stealing or any other gross offense, he was required to wear an empty barrel turned over his head, with his head through a hole cut in the bottom of the barrel with the word "thief" written in large capitals on the back of the barrel. He was then required to walk a certain beat for several hours and some times at "double quick."

If for a minor offense, he was required to carry a billet of wood on his shoulders.

If a fellow refused to walk as he was ordered, a cord was tied around his thumbs and he was drawn up to a beam to a "tip toe" until he was completely exhausted. This is said to be the most cruel punishment of all.

On one occasion, I saw a man taken to a pump and held down and the water pumped on his head and in his face till he was almost drowned.

Sometimes I wished that I could identify the fellow that stole my blanket or my rations the first night after I came to prison.

I never could see the use of violating the law, either civil or military, therefore I believe I retained the good will of my officers during the entire war, and my civil officers until the present time.

But one night I had a trying experience which now comes vividly to my mind. Tom Grice, one of my bunk mates, was taken very ill at a late hour, and in addition to his other ills, cramp colic seized upon him and her suffered great agony.

He asked me to do something for him, but I had nothing to do with. But there was a small doctor shop standing near the center of the prison where a small supply of drugs were kept, and sometimes a physician remained there at night.

But how could I manage to get there? was a question. I knew that it was a violation of the rules for one to be seen outside the barracks after taps, or even to have a light inside.

Our barracks was situated near the parapet, upon which a sentinel walked, and it would be impossible for me to go to the shop without his notice and I would subject myself to be shot; and I also knew that a prisoner was not allowed to speak to a sentinel; neither was a sentinel allowed to speak to a prisoner.

But I felt it my duty to seek relief for a suffering comrade.

I had run through a shower of bullets upon the filed as a courier, and under the circumstances I determined to risk my life again for Tom.

So I went to the door, opened it very cautiously and looked for the sentry, and on seeing him near I ventured to speak to him, telling him of my sick friend and my desire to go for medicine, and to my surprise and relief he kindly replied "all right."

I then ran through the bleak wind and snow with my bare feet, secured the medicine and returned unhurt, except a little chilly.

That sentinel was a man with a kind heart, although he wore a blue coat, very different from one of whom I will speak before the close of this narrative.

At the beginning of this story I said that our rations were issued to us individually—every fellow taking care of his own, but after a while the plan was changed which proved to be a little better.

There was a room built at the end of each barracks in which a furnace was made to cook our rations when they were issued to us raw.

We were divided into messes of twenty four men each. These messes elected their own cook who received the rations for his mess and divided to each man twice a day—there being too little to make three meals.

The cooks were furnished with a tin plate, tin cup, and a knife for each man of their several messes. Our meat consisted of beef only. Some days we drew hard tacks, some days meal, some days flour and some days light bread.

We could have eaten one day's rations at one time and quit hungry.

My mess instructed our cook to take the crust of the bread, parch it and make coffee of it.

This left us about one mouthful of bread to eat with the two mouthsful /mouthfuls/ of meat, but was a little better to eat than to eat the crust without the coffee.

I don't know how I would like bread coffee now but it was mighty good then.

The most palatable dish we had was when our cook would boil the beef and stir in the meat and make a kind of greasy mush. Each fellow got a whole spoonful at once and we thought it was really the best thing we had ever eaten. I thought then if I ever got home I would have as much of it as I wanted, but some how I have had no desire for it since.

One day as I was strolling around in the prison for recreation, I met up with John Geiger, whom I knew in by gone days.

He was a native of Bryan County /Georgia/ and had gone to Florida before the war, and enlisted in a Florida regiment and captured sometime before I was.

I was truly glad to see him notwithstanding the adverse circumstances under which we met.

John was a noble fellow, but his health was very poor, and he was soon confined to his quarters where I went to see him several times.

I do not know what became of him, but as I learned that he never reached home, the supposition is he died in that Federal prison as an honorable prisoner of war.[11]

I also met up with William Strickling, another Bryan County boy. He belonged to the 25th Georgia Regiment, a noble band of Confederates who distinguished themselves on many battle fields.

Billy was a splendid fellow. He once lived at my father's and I knew him intimately.

He came to my barracks several times during our stay, and as we talked of the past—how we worked and played together, rehearsing amusing incidents, etc., we would almost forget our present surrounding.

In this place I learned that it is useless to believe half you hear. It is man's nature to lie, and if he is void of all moral restraint, he is apt to give his nature full swing. Sometimes a fellow, to create a little sensation, he would tell that we were soon to be exchanged, and that he had overheard some Yankees talking, and in almost no time the glad news was spread all over the prison when in reality there was no foundation for the report.

If someone expressed his thoughts, it would be told as a fact by someone else, and the Sergeant Plum was asked about it he would say that he had said no such thing.

If anything were told, before it got half around the place it was added to or changed so that it was quite a different tale.

Just so it is today. If anyone, on account of jealousy or envy, or any other cause speaks disparagingly of another, by the time it goes a mile or so it is changed into a slanderous lie. A lie travels much faster than the truth.

Sometime in the month of January, I think it was, a little better day dawned upon us.

A sutler[12] shop was established just outside with a little window opening into the prison and the little money which had been taken from the prisoners on entering was given them in checks on the sutler.

These checks were of different denominations, ranging from five to fifty cents.

Some of the prisoners whose homes were inside the Federal lines were allowed to write home and their families or friends could send them a small amount if they chanced to have any U.S. currency.

But, we, whose homes were beyond the lines, could get none, as our people possessed Confederate money only and it was not current there in Yankeedom.

A five cent check would buy a quart of meal or a few Irish potatoes, and once in a while a fellow could take his fill of hoe cakes or boiled potatoes without seasoning.

A few times I saw men who had no checks picking up potato peelings and eating them which had been thrown away by those who were fortunate enough to be able to buy them.

We could but envy those fortunate ones. But after awhile we learned that "where there is a will there is a way."

Some ingenious fellow conceived a plan. He procured a small amount, went to the sutler and bought a small file and a pair of pincers. He then cut or filled teeth in the back of his case knife which served as a saw: then taking a piece of beef bone, holding it with his pincers, he proceeded to saw it into thin strips.

He then filed or cut these in proper shape, riveted them to-gether, forming a complete tooth pick with blades and handle. These picks he bartered to the sutler for meal.

Many of us took up the trade and in a short time I could make fancy article by polishing them with sand paper and engraving letters or some fancy design on the handles.

After considerable practice, I could make picks which I could sell for a five cent check each.

We would also buy guttapercha[13] buttons and convert them into finger rings. Some of these we made plain and some fancy by inserting silver sets of different designs. I think I became an expert in the business.

But finally we "glutted the market" and they were dull sale.

Sometimes a fellow could, on the sly, make a trade with a guard for tobacco if nothing more. I had no use for tobacco myself, but there were men there who suffered intensely for it.

I seldom sold rings or picks myself but would get someone else to trade for me.

I remember on one occasion, Sam Zouks, one of my bunk mates took several rings and tooth picks which he had secured from different parties, strung them on a string and approached near the "dead line" and softly asked the sentinel if he would purchase them.

The sentinel told him to throw them up to him and if he liked them he would buy them. Sam tied them to a stick and tossed them to a Yankee. The scoundrel put them in his pocket, and pointing his gun at Sam, ordered him to "mark time." Of course, Sam had it to do and the Yank kept his rings.

Had the prisoners been armed, that rascal would have been riddled with bullets for indignation ran high all over the prison.

There is a feeling like unto kinship among soldiers. If one is imposed upon by an outsider, they will resent it for him and stick to him like a twin brother.

I have seen soldiers have disputes and be almost at dagger's point, but when thrown in line of battle to meet the foe, they would cheer and speak words of encouragement to each other as though nothing had ever been wrong between them.

There was some clothing issued to some when they made it appear they were about to go naked. This clothing was second hands goods, and some out-of-date goods which were not stylish for the northern gentry to wear.

The coat given as were perfect novelties. They were of black material, short waist with long narrow forked tails, reaching down nearly to the ankles. Our old folks remember that these coats were fashionable before the war but had gone out of style. The tails of these coats were cut off (most of them) before they were given us which left but a short jacket which lacked about an inch or more reaching down to the waist of the pants.

The cold wind seemed to know just where this vacant place was and sometimes a fellow would feel just like his body was being cut in twain.

I drew no clothes myself except a pair of pants, but I secured one of these jackets from a fellow by giving him a hoe cake and a tooth pick.

This fellow had either stolen these articles from some fellow prisoner, or had drawn twice from the quartermaster by changing his name and representing himself as being naked.

It was real funny to see the boys stepping around over the prison with these short jackets on.

Sometime in February, it was rumored again that an exchange had been agreed upon by the Federal and Confederate authorities, but there had been so many false reports that we put no confidence in the rumor.

One day however, two officers came inside the prison and to each barracks beating up for volunteers to enlist in the Federal cavalry and go west to fight Indians.[14]

They insisted that it would be better for us to do this as it was doubtful as to when, if ever, we would be exchanged.

We took this as a favorable indication, and that there was an exchange soon to take place. I don't think they succeeded in securing a single volunteer from the whole prison.

A few days after this, we saw three officers walk up on the parapet from the outside between prison 1 and prison 2, one of whom bearing a large roll of paper in his hand.

When they reached the center beat, one of them cried out "Oh yes! Oh yes!"

Every prisoner in the two prisons who was able to run rushed around with a yell that made the welkin /?/ ring.

Yes, the cooks left the kitchens and the wash house was evacuated and the bunks gave up the sick—all that were able, and they, too, joined in the throng.

When quiet was restored, the officer, with a loud a distinct voice, said that he would take a squad of 500 men from that prison to go on exchange, and in a few days he would take 500 more, and so on until all were exchanged.

Such a wild demonstration of joy I never witnessed. This demonstration was conclusive evidence that every one had rather join the Confederate army than remain in prison.

The officer then announced that he would call by states and by date of capture. As he called a name he was required to give the letter of his company, number of his regiment and state to which he belonged.

To my surprise, I found that some had been there more than six months longer than I had; and I soon found that I would fail to get out on that call.

In about a week more, another squad of 500 was called for and the date of my capture not reached yet, but I thought surely my name would be reached next call.

Another week passed and no call for another squad and the time passed slowly by, but at the end of the second week—sometime in March—the third squad was called.

The Georgia captives were called down nearly to my date, but they took up another state and called to the same date and then finally took up another state and so on.

Finally they took up Georgia again and called to the date of my capture, and the last man called was W.P. Merritt of my regiment who was captured the same time myself. I was sure then that my time would be next, but the next never came.

We could get no information and ever at a loss to know the cause of the suspension.

As I have already said, we could hear rumors of all kinds. One of these rumors was that the contending armies had so vigorously renewed hostilities until the exchange had been broken off. We found that it was broken off and stayed "broken off."

Some time after this, it was announced to us that the exchange had "been broken off" sure enough and a proposition was made to us.

It was proposed to us that all prisoners who would take the oath of allegiance to the U.S. and remain north of the Ohio River, they would be released on that proviso. Some few agreed to this proposition. One of them told me that it was his intention to get his release and then escape to South America, as he did not propose to live in Yankeedom.

All those who accepted this proposition were put in prison 2 and the rest of us were crowded into prison 3.

I don't think that a single Georgian remained in prison 2 under this proposition in fact very few of any state.

All of my company and most of my regiment secured quarters together in barracks 3. This was about the last of March and at times the weather became a little moderate, though at times it was severely cold.

We still suffered much from hunger as well as from cold, but as I have already said, some of us at times could assuage our hunger by securing some meal from the sutler.

One day after I had secured three five cent checks, I started to the sutler, and on my way I noticed a group of men who seemed much interested in something, and as I drew near to them, I found they were playing what they called "chuckleluck."/chuck-a-luck/[15]

I watched them awhile and concluded that I would try my hand. I thought that I had discovered the lucky number, and felt certain that I could double my money with perfect ease. So I laid down one of my checks on that number and behold, I lost it.

I felt like I was ruined and turned off to leave. But then I thought of the old adage, "if you fail, try, try, again" and turned back and laid another check on the same number, feeling confident that I would get my money back this time, but lo, and behold! I lost the second time.

This seemed more than I could bear and I started back to my barracks: but then I recalled to mind the old saying that "it's a long lane that never turns," so I felt like it was time for this lane to turn, and that I would risk my last check—that I would "make or break."

So I went back and laid down my last check and lost that, too. I went back to my barracks, covered up myself and repented of my folly. This was my last experience in gambling, and this act I kept secret until now.

As the weather moderated, sickness decreased. Smallpox was a thing of the past, and we felt no fear of that dread disease.

But oh, how much anxiety we felt as to our future. We could hear nothing from our homes nor from our comrades in the army; still occasionally a captive from our forces came as a supplement to our already crowded prison, but they could tell us nothing of importance. Some times however, a newspaper or two was thrown into the prison containing "news from the front," which, in every case was discouraging to our armies. But we had learned not to believe every newspaper report, and we also thought that this discouraging news was given us to tantalize and to induce us to take the oath of allegiance, but we all stood firm, resigning ourselves to the consequences, whether they be weal or woe.

It is true we suffered severely both mentally and physically, yet there were some amusing incidents which served as a little passtime.

Mr. Goodall, the big and fat man, who came to us from Tennessee the day before our capture, whom I have already mentioned remained with us during our entire stay in this place of confinement, true to his convictions as to right and wrong.

He had been very corpulent, but was now reduced to almost a mere skeleton, but retained his health, and was always jovial and afforded much amusement for all with whom he mingled.

Were it not for jolly people this world would be ten fold worse that it is.

He, too, suffered much from hunger and cold, but said he suffered more for tobacco than anything else. After he would give part of his scanty rations for a chew from those who chanced to get a little from the other.

In our barracks, we held moot courts occasionally—Goodall acting as judge. If a fellow did anything which we conceived to be wrong, he was arranged /arraigned/ before the court and tried.

These cases were of a criminal nature and seldom failed of conviction, but the convict was seldom ever required to pay the penalty.

These courts afforded a little amusement and passtime, but the time passed off very slowly apparently.

Sometimes the boys would sit upon their bunks and sing some good old religious songs, and at other times were songs such as "Bonnie Blue Flag," "Dixie," and "When Thus Cruel War Is Over," etc.

Well do I remember Noah McHenry, an Alabamian who was always jovial and singing some love song—one of which was "Oh la gals, do pitty my case for I am getting old and wrinkle in the face."

How glad I would be to meet those who suffered with me in that terrible place, but most of them have passed to the great beyond.

Sometime we were informed that General Lee had surrendered himself and his army to General Grant. This was sad news to us and we could scarcely realize that it was true.

For my own part, I thought if Lee had surrendered the balance of the Confederate armies would have to follow suit and that the failure of the South was inevitable, and if this be the case, let the inevitable come at once that we may be released from that awful place of confinement.

A little later on we heard that some clever fellow had cut President Lincoln's throat.

On hearing this there was some misgivings on the part of some, but as to my own part at that time I was truly glad for it for if any man or set of men merited my hatred it was Lincoln and his counselors for it was they who had been waging war against a people who were struggling for their liberties which they deemed dearer than life.

There is no man in the nation who can convince me that the cause of the South was an unrighteous cause. Right does not prevail every time.

If a big man jumps on a little fellow and gives him a whipping, it is no proof that the big fellow was right and the little fellow was wrong.

Time passed slowly by. I knew that it was time for the trees to be budding and the flowers to be blooming and the grass to be growing and all nature to be smiling outside, but when, oh when could I see these things.

Sometime later on we found by climbing up on the joists of the building and looking through the cracks of the gable, we could see at a distance large fields of grain, green and beautiful. And we could see men plowing, so far away that they appeared as very small moving objects.

I felt that it would be a treat and recreation to go plough for some man for as much as I could eat.

About this time, we learned that those few men whom we left in prison (when we were put in prison 3) under conditions of their taking the oath of allegiance and being released and remaining north of the Ohio River, were still in prison.

Why this was I never learned, but I was right glad that they were no better off than we.

For sometime nothing occurred to break the monotony of the situation. But sometime in the month of May our mess cook became sick and it was necessary for us to elect another.

So one of my mess, a North Georgian by the name of Childs, came to me and asked me if I would accept the position.

I was somewhat astounded and scarcely knew how to answer the question. I must now confess that I was somewhat anxious for the place for I thought that the cook, by skimming the pot and picking up the crumbs, could assuage their hunger a little and never be censured.

But I managed to suppress my anxiety, and told my kind friend that if my mess desired my services I would do for them the best that I could.

I soon found out that I had an opponent whose name I have forgotten, but he was a Texan and a good and clever fellow, too. He seemed determined on getting the place.

I lay upon my bunk while the campaign waged warm for an hour or more. They had no whiskey to electioneer with as office seekers have here now.

Neither did they have money to buy votes, but it seemed that the campaign was conducted in an honorable way. The election was held and I was declared elected by a good majority.

The position of cook is not a desirable one ordinarily, but in that place it was considered a boon.

I went into the kitchen, and strange to say, I suffered very little from hunger while there, although I acted honestly with my men, divided the rations equally, taking not even a crumb above my share.

The weather had considerably moderated by this time, but even the month of May was quite cold for a South Georgian with a bob-tail coat and thin pants and almost no shoes. But as I had access to the kitchen, I fared moderately well as to cold.

A few weeks later, we could hear rumors of all kind in regard to the probability of our being released.

If a fellow told anything, before it reached half way across the prison, it was changed into quite a different tale.

But it was evident that all our soldiery had succumbed to the inevitable and it seemed reasonable that we would soon be released.

We waited in suspense and anxiety until the 11th day of June, when two officers appeared on the parapet and with loud voice cried: "Attention!" Then a yell went up from all parts of the prison and every fellow rushed around to hear what was up.

When all was quiet one of them told us that we would be released on parole as rapidly as possible. So at once they began to call, and I was almost the first one called.

Soon all of my date of capture were called and we were ushered in and through a kind of office, and after being measured, etc., we received our papers; and passing out through a commissary, we received two day's rations which consisted of a small piece of bacon and a few hard tacks.

We walked out and on to the city. But when we got to the suburbs a few of us concluded to stop and take our square meal if it took all our two day's rations..

We ate about half and concluded to quit and hurry on to the city where we were to get transportation tickets.

After procuring tickets to Cincinnati we waited some time before our train left, and while waiting there several citizens came and talked to us, several of whom were farmers who tried to hire us to remain and work for them on the farm. Everyone declined the offer, and we joined in singing "Dixie."

"Oh, Dixieland is a land of clover,

When we die, we die all over.

Look away, look away, look away, look away,

Away down South in Dixie, away, away,

In Dixieland I take my stand

To live and die in Southern land.

Away, away, away down South in Dixie."

We were soon on our way Southward and just two weeks from that day we reached Savannah, Georgia, from which place some of us had to walk to our homes. My house was just 44 miles.

A Coincidence

The readers of the foregoing narrative are aware that I, with some others of my regiment (5th Georgia Cavalry) were captured near Mufreesboro, Tennessee, and among the captives was Matthew Miller of Company E of our regiment, and who is a well known citizen of Bulloch County.

Our horses were captured, too, and, of course, became property of the U.S. Government. This was the 6th day of September, 1864.

We were carried to Camp Chase, near the city of Columbus, Ohio, and there held as prisoners of war until we were released by parole on the 11th day of June, 1865.

Mr. Miller reached his home about the 25th of the same month, and to his great delight found his horse at home in his lot, the very identical horse which had been captured with himself by the enemy near 10 months before.

Now the question will naturally arise with some as to how the horse came there.

Well it happened this way: P.C. Hagins, a stepson of Mr. Miller, who was quite a youth then, had served a short time in the war, and honorably discharged at the surrender, while on his way home through the county of Burke, this state, saw the horse and recognized him as being the same horse his stepfather rode to war.

Cone made inquiry of the man as to how he came in possession of him and was told that the Yankee cavalry had left him there as a broken down horse, and that he was now the proper owner. Cone laid claim to him but was refused.

He came home and with the shrewdness of a man obtained witnesses, went and identified the horse and led him home to the great delight of the family.

But while they rejoiced at getting the horse again, they were grieved at not knowing the fate of the rider, their father and husband: neither did they know until Mr. Miller reached home the time stated above.

Much kindness was lavished upon Jack (for that was his name) and he soon became a serviceable horse again, and lived to do the family faithful work until he died at the age of 24 years.

I doubt there being a survivor of the war North or South, who can tell a similar tale and substantiate it by living witnesses.

Notes:

[1] Pember, Phoebe Yates. *A Southern Woman's Story: Life in Confederate Richmond.* (Marietta, Georgia: Mockingbird Books, reprint 1994)

[2] For an insightful discourse about Civil War prisons see, Hesseltine, William B. *Civil War Prisons: A Study in War Psychology.* (Ohio State University Press, 1930)

[3] Barbiere, Joe, *Scraps from the Prison Table at Camp Chase and Johnson's Island.* (Doylestown, PA, 1868) included in Hesseltine, p. 52.

[4] Dorsey is mistaken, General Johnston was removed from command and replaced by General Hood on July 17, 1864, six weeks before Atlanta fell to Union forces.

[5] It became common practice during the Civil War for the cavalry to fight both mounted and dismounted. In this respect, they served more as mounted infantry than the heavy cavalry or dragoons of previous wars. Once dismounted, one out of every four troopers was left behind to hold his horse and the horses of three other troopers. Therefore, every dismounted unit saw a logical reduction of 25% of its effective fighting force. Yet, this new use of cavalry was highly effective and mobile and was later adopted by Union forces. This new strategy of cavalry was primarily developed by Gen. Wheeler from experience gained in operations in

Kentucky in 1862 and 1863, where he wrote, while in the field, *A Revised System of Cavalry Tactics for the Use of the Cavalry and Mounted Infantry, C.S.A.*

[6] Bushwhackers (ambushers) were particularly active in pro-Union East Tennessee. See "Longstreet at Knoxville," by E. Porter Alexander, Brigadier-General, C.S.A., *Battles and Leaders of the Civil War*, vol. III, 745

[7] A low over shoe made of rubber.

[8] As early as the fall of 1861 Confederate prisoners were freezing to death. Prison officials promised to provide heat by stoves, but three years passed before any provisions were made. *Official Records*, ser. 2, vol. I, 544.

[9] Attempts were made by some Columbus citizens to help the prisoners, but they were usually turned away. "It is but justice to the ladies of Columbus to say that they offered to furnish comfortable beds and bedding for us but were denied the privilege by the commandant because he said it was not permitted by the orders. When these kind-hearted ladies visited us in our vile prison and beheld our wretched condition they involuntarily broke into tears. They gave us all they were permitted to bestow—their sympathy and tears...." A.J. Morey (former Camp Chase prisoner) to the Editor of the Cynthia, Ky. News, Dec. 11, 1861, *Official Records*, ibid, 545.

[10] Fred Williams, private Company D, 5th Georgia Cavalry died on February 22, 1865. T.F. Linder, Private Company D, 5th Georgia Cavalry died February 6, 1865. They are buried at Camp Chase Confederate Cemetery in Columbus, Ohio, with 2,087 fellow Confederate soldiers. 308 were from Georgia. Other members of the 5th Georgia Cavalry that died while imprisoned at Camp Chase: George W. Lane, private Company B; J.M. Mears, sergeant Company F; A.J. Phillips, private Company H; B.H. Spencer, private Company H; Luke Rozier, rank unknown Company K.

[11] John Geiger, private Company G, 7th Florida Infantry, died while imprisoned at Camp Chase on June 12, 1865, exactly two months after Lee's surrender at Appomattox.

[12] Sutlers were used in both Union and Confederate armies. They were civilians, approved by the army, that sold various goods and wares (books, newspapers, food, tobacco, and at times alcohol,

though officially prohibited) to the soldiers. They usually made camp with the soldiers. Yet, if allowed in prison camps, the sutler's list of goods was menial at best.

[13] Guttapercha buttons were made of hard rubber.

[14] The Federal government offered Confederate prisoners of war the opportunity to sign an oath of allegiance to the United States Government and then serve in the Federal cavalry. At first they were required to fight against their former Confederate comrades, but policy was changed and they served in the west fighting Indians. Those who chose this option were soon nicknamed, "Galvinized Yankees," bearing a coat of Union blue on the outside while remaining Rebels on the inside. Only 6,000 of the approximate 220,000 Confederates taken prisoner served in this capacity.

[15] Chuck-a-luck was a gambling game played with cards and dice. See Wiley, Bell Irvin. *The Life of Johnny Reb: The Common Soldier of the Confederacy*. (Louisiana State University Press, 1943), 37.

6

Confederate War Record of Z.T. DeLoach

Z. Taylor DeLoach joined the 5th Georgia Cavalry while still in his teens. Yet, he experienced the struggles and hardships of war as much as any who were his senior.

He had at least two steeds shot out from under him, forged furlough papers to get a chance to visit home, and was captured and subsequently made a prisoner of war.

DeLoach was from Bulloch County, Georgia, and served in the Confederate army along with his father, a captain of state troops, and three brothers. After the war DeLoach and his brother, Robert William Deloach, also a member of the 5th Georgia Cavalry (see photo), built and operated DeLoach's Mill and constructed dams for people who wanted ponds. He became commander of the Cone Camp, U.V.C., and finally died at home on February 16, 1933. He was the next to the last surviving Confederate veteran in Bulloch county.

In the fall of 1862, I joined the State Troops and my father was elected Captain and George P. Haveron, Colonel. We were sent to No. 7, on what was the Gulf R.R., now the Seaboard. We drilled there about 3 months, when I became ill with rheumatism and finally got a discharge from war service. I came home and stayed three months and I got so anxious about the war I wanted to go back and be with the boys as I was too young to care anything about the girls; not near so much as I have since then. So I went to the cavalry and got in by lying a little and swearing I would not try to get out on account of my age and broken arm. We were stationed at Isle of Hope. We drilled there about three months and were sent to Charleston, S.C. to picket[1] Sullivan's Island and other places. We stayed there 6 or 8 months and were then sent to Cedar Creek, Fla., near Jacksonville. We stayed there a very short while and saw a little of what war was. Had one little skirmish while there and was sent to the front. There it was war all the time, retreating and fighting. When we got to the Chattahoochee River,[2] I was chosen with others, about twenty in number, to hold the blue jackets back until our folks could cross the river and destroy the crossing. We boys that did get out swam the river about night, found our command and had a good night's rest. Nut /sic/ while we were resting the Yanks were planting artillery on the other side and got us well located. About daybreak they shelled out. They killed Marion Miller. I think that was the first man our Company lost. We kept up our retreat till we neared Atlanta. There about 300 of us were detailed and ordered to report to Gen. Robinson. He took us in back of the Yankee lines to tear up all R.R.s and bridges and cut off all communication that we could. I tell you the Yankees sure kept us moving six days and nights. We didn't take the saddles off our horses. We ro/a/sted enough for ourselves for one day. There were no other rations except sometimes the farmers gave us what food they had cooked. We had several bad fights on the raid and lost lots of our men.

At Salt Lake, Va.[3] I was left in behind the Yankees lines with John Neal and Leon Neal of Thomas, Co. /county/, David Glisson of Tattnall Co., and Mike Parrish of Millen /Georgia/. The two were latter /sic/ killed, but part of us finally got back in our own lines. Then the boys began to get furloughs. By the time the command got to Waynesboro,[4] Burke Co., Ga. all had been home but J.N. Mikell, James Rimes and myself. They had quit giving furloughs, so we decided to come anyway. We forged our papers, but got thru /sic/ all right and were at home when the Yankees passed our way. The next day, Brother John and I decided to go across Black Creek where we thought they had passed, when we got over, we met the old man John Goodman and talked to him awhile. Then we went to Mal Hagins to see what they had done. While we were talking to them we looked down the road and saw at least forty men coming in a big hurry. They had horses, mules, food, and everything they had taken from people along the route. They were going back to camp so they had us penned. I thought I did not see any way to get out so we rode to meet them and rode up in ten feet of them.

I told the leaders to surrender but they said they had plenty of men behind them. I told him we did too. While we were talking, he pulled his pistol and I, too, started to fire, but my gun would not shoot.[5] About that time they all began shooting. John said if my gun would not fire, we had better leave, so we started off. As I turned they hit my horse in the side and in the head, so he went but a short distance before he fell dead. But we had turned them back and sent them about six miles. I then took the saddle off my horse and footed it home. About a week later the army passed I started around them to our own army and found them at Green Pond, S.C. The officer was mighty nice to me but I was detailed for picket duty that night. That was all the punishment I got. We did not stay there long, before we took up our march to keep out of the Yankees' way. We soon got as far as Columbia, S.C. There I was detailed again and left on the side of the bridge back of the Yanks' till our folks got across the river. We stayed as we could in safety and then turned to run but found the bridge afire. It was a double bridge, walled in, so I put my hat over my face and ran thru /sic/ the fire. Some others did the same and we got thru all right except where our clothes were burned some. Some jumped in the river and swam across, some did not cross and were captured. We that did cross stayed there near the river, and fought the Yankees awhile, then marched on, they pursuing us. At every chance, we would form a line and fight 'till they began to flank us, which they could do well, as they had plenty of men to entertain us in front and an army to go around us on each side. Of course, we had to resume our march. When we got into N.C. Wade Hampton, the Senior Cavalry General, bunched up what cavalry he could and cut out to surprise the Yankees while they were in camp. We rode all night, swam two rivers, reached their camp by daybreak. They were surrounded by branches but we found a trail to cross one and went over two abreast, one going up the brouch /sic/, the other down. Soon we closed in on them and took those that were in bed and some that were up. By the time we had things going our way, the infantry, camped near by, started in on us and ran us out. In that fight they shot my mule down and I ran to get one of the Yankees' horses, but before I could unhitch it they shot that. I heeled it from there to the branch, but I could not get a ride and I had to get to one side and let all pass, the Yankees too. That night we came to an old man's house by the name of McBean. He treated us mighty nice, fed us on Johnny cakes, the first I ever saw. They had a piece of board that they stood on its edge in front of the fire, and when it got hot they put the dough on it and baked it. I enjoyed it after fasting all day. He gave us a good bed to sleep on something we were not used to and after breakfast he gave us directions to Johnson's Ferry, near Fayetteville. The bridge there was burned so he gave us a new cut. But we did not get far before the Yankees got there and he put them right on out tracks. Of course, they took us into their hotels at Fayetteville for the night. Next morning, their General sent for us. They carried us up there and asked a few questions, then told the guards to take us out, I understood, some one had told them our men had stripped their men of clothing and I think they must have. Soon after we got back to camp, orders came to take our shoes, hats, and coats off and burn them. That was done and a little later, we were on the march. It was sleeting, and I had not walked much in a long time. My feet were sore cold but we marched right in the road behind all the horses and wagons, the mud half foot deep. We marched three days, this way before we got to a railroad. There, they shipped us to the coast, Newbern, N.C. The next day, they loaded us for prison, Hart's Island, about 50 or 60 miles above N.Y. city. There they fed us on six soda crackers and a very small piece of meat a day. I did not get hungry but once in awhile. We were soon paroled, they took us to N.Y. city and gave us a square meal which lasted 'till I got home. Otherwise they treated me as well as I could have expected. My time in prison was from March 12 to June 12, 1865. I had a tough time. My dinner in N.Y. made me sick. As long as I could ride I got along very well, but walking got away with me. When we landed on the island the Yankees soldiers gave me a pair of shoes and I sold part of my crackers and bought me a coat. I finally got home O.K. and have grumbled about food ever since

Notes:

[1] Picketing consisted primarily of guarding against actions of the enemy.

[2] The Chattahoochee River is located just north of Atlanta and was the last natural barrier between Sherman and the city. Federal forces crossed the Chattahoochee on July 9, 1864, after battling Confederate forces for a number of days.

[3] DeLoach's narrative jumps from the middle of the Atlanta Campaign to after Atlanta's fall and the detachment of Wheeler's cavalry to east Tennessee and southern Virginia.

[4] See chapter 4 for a description of the fighting around Waynesboro.

[5] By the outbreak of the Civil War technology had greatly improved side arms. Samuel Colt had recently developed his six shot .36 Colt Navy revolver and .44 Colt Army revolver, and soon many other manufacturers followed suit. Despite their versatility in the field, these new styles of revolvers still used black powder, perscussion cap and ball, and were prone to jamming and misfiring.

7

Capture - Remount Detachment of the Liberty Troop

Raymond Cay's exciting account of avoiding capture by Union troops occurred late in the war. Sherman had already passed through most of Georgia and was in Bulloch County near Savannah. Bulloch County suffered mercilessly at the hands of Sherman's left wing made up of the 20th Corps. They met little resistance...

Retreating before Sherman's push to the coast, dismounted members of the troop were given short furloughs to go home by train to get fresh horses. Lt. Stevens took command and returning, met the advanced cavalry of our enemies at Bulloch County.

We began picking up numbers of their foragers and house burners and soon had more prisoners that we had men. By riding hard day and night we put our prisoners on the tender of the last train to leave McIntosh station before the destruction of the railroad, in the care of Remsheart's company.

Returning to the front we crossed the Canoochee River and met their cavalry. The bridge was burned behind us; we had to swim our horses, the weather freezing! Falling in with Captain John Wiberly of the 29th Georgia Battalion, a fine soldier and gentleman, he took command of our detachment.

That day two couriers from Remsheart's company, Sam Baker and Charlie Quarterman, met us. They had a dispatch from Colonel Hood, written by his adjutant, Lt. Rainey, to meet him at Walthourville where he expected to give battle the next day. Colonel Hood, as all old citizens know, was doing Coastal duty in the counties of Liberty and McIntosh.

We were all cheered by this good news as we hurried on our way. Encumbered by more prisoners, we turned them loose. Before midnight we reached Taylor's Creek and stopped to see the King family, refugees from Colonel's Island. One of their boys, Clarence, was with us. I fell asleep on the lounge, the boys were trying to wake me. I heard the sound of a dear little woman's voice, Mrs. Roswell King, Jr.; "Oh, please don't wake him; see how tired he is! Poor little boy, let him sleep. Please let him sleep a little bit longer." The smile on my face brought a laugh from the boys, and we were off! As we reached the old Midway road, on the outskirts of the village, we could see in the deep sandy road fresh signs of cavalry and camp fires at the Nettle Branch.

We halted. My brother, J.D. Cay, advised Captain Wiberly not to report to Hood at such an ungodly hour, but to divide the squad, a part going to our home and the rest to Colonel Quarterman's, whose three sons were also of our party. By doing so, we could all get a good breakfast and some sleep. It was then about one hour before daylight; so we turned to the right, crossed the new road branch and were at home! My father was upstairs in bed. The family had refugeed. Captain Winn was with my father. The servants were soon busy getting breakfast. I remember passing through the breakfast room and seeing a long table shining with silver, all of it soon to go into Yankee pockets.

I must digress here to say the camp fires we saw at the Nettle branch were not the fires of Hood's Battalion as he promised in his dispatch. They belonged to Captain Hancock and a large detachment of his regiment, the 9th Pennsylvania Cavalry. Day was breaking. My brother had gone over to Quarterman's to wake the boys and bring them to breakfast. He was standing, talking to them, all in one room downstairs on mattresses thrown on the floor, and with their clothes on.

/?/ voice saying "Don't trouble dat hoss! Don't trouble dat hoss, I tell you! Dat's Mass Josie hoss!" He opened the door and saw old Tie struggling with a yankee soldier to save "Mass Josie's hoss!! The yard was full, the house surrounded by yankee cavalry! Not a gun was fired! Our boys were prisoners!

At my home, some of the boys rode away before I knew of any danger. Captain Winn, crippled with rhumatism, tried to mount a horse to go and save the boys; but falling, he tried to walk with his cane. They grabbed him, too! My father, very excitedly, called to me to wait for Mr. Fennell who was in bed upstairs. He had been shot through the body at Kenessaw Mountain. Bullets were dropping in the yard and hitting the stable. The boy was helping me saddle my horse, a bunch of yelling, charging yankees were nearing the open gate as Thorpy Varnedoe, firing his carbine, and Mr. Jenkins, his pistol, rushed through. Trying to follow them, two Yanks blocked my way. Jumping from my horse and hugging the big gate post, I poked my gun up at them, holding my fire; remembering at the instant how the white men kept the Indians away in the story books. It worked here, too, for they stopped emptying their pistols; they turned to run!

My father, standing near, continued to say: "Wait for Mr. Fennell!" I put the fine sights of my carbine in the back of a big dutchman not ten yards away. I could hit a rat at the distance! The thought came to me, I can get away if I kill him; they will get Pa and burn the house! Raising to the top of his head, I fired and in the cold, clear morning I heard my ball hit the church! My horse was gone; the boy met me with him; I was up and gone; many foes coming—charging, yelling, shouting—I could not escape by the way of the others. Running my horse deep in the branch and leaving him afoot, I was safe!

Captain Wimberly and his two aides were captured, and, of the Liberty Troop, Lt. Willie Stevens, Corporal J.D. Cay, Gus, Joe and Willie Quarterman, Clarence King, Henry Porter Stevens, and others, I think, that I can recall. They took Captain Winn to Midway and turned him loose when they learned he was not a combatant. Our boys were sent to Pt. Lookout prison,[1] freed in June, 1865, sent to Richmond, and walked home. All railroads had been destroyed.

The next time I saw my father he showed me his hat, - a yankee bullet had passed through the top.

Where was Colonel Hood and his men who were to fight that day? Sam Baker and Charles Quarterman told me after the war they were sleeping in the woods at the end of Baker's lane. With

Colonel Hood, they were awakened by the firing, mounted their horses, left at a run and never stopped until they reached Johnston Station, and continued up the river road. These boys were his couriers, lived on and near Baker's lane and knew what they were talking about.

Captain Hancock mounted his prisoners, continued on to Johnston Station, turned up the railroad, burned a trestle and returned to his camp at the Nettle branch the same night.

If Hood's Battalion ever fired a shot at a Yankee in Liberty County, I have never been able to find out where it was. Poor fellows, they were outnumbered 50 to 1. He had many fine men and boys. Everbody was fleeing before Sherman's great army of 65,000 veteran soldiers, the South had spent its last dollar, sent its old man and little boys to fight its battles, defeat was in the air, all hope was gone. The Christmas days had come but all our joys had turned to tears. Our beloved southland was doomed.

R. Cay
Late Liberty Independent
Troop

An Addenda

With all our bad luck, one thing happened that day that always gives me joy to remember. The night was freezing, December 13th, 1864, a raw winter. My brother had loaned me his great overcoat of English make, received through blockade. It hung over my saddle in my wild ride; it fell off, a Yankee soldier picked it up. My brother told him it was his coat and, when he proved it by the other prisoners, he gave it to him! Dave often told me that coat kept him from freezing to death that horrid winter in prison when so many poor boys died in the cold.

Respectfully,
R. Cay

Notes:

[1] Point Lookout was located at Point Lookout, Maryland, and was the largest prisoner of war camp in the North. No barracks were provided and the men slept in tents. Water was often scarce, and the same brutality that existed in other Civil War prison camps also plagued Point Lookout.

8

Letters of Orlando Devant Chester, 5th Georgia Cavalry

Of the 11 letters written by Chester in this work, 6 were written during the Atlanta Campaign. The first letter written from the Atlanta area was on June 30, 1864, from Marietta. The 5th Georgia Cavalry had recently been dispatched to the Army of Tennessee commanded by General Joseph Johnston. The Atlanta Campaign primarily consisted of bold, defensive measures under Johnston. Overwhlemed numerically, Johnston would dig in and fortify a position, only to fall back and reconstruct fortifications once again. Though some considered Johnston's defensive measures brilliant, President Davis did not and he lost his command to General Hood.

It was the constant fighting and hardships of the Atlanta Campaign that so depleted the ranks of the 5th Georgia. After the fall of Atlanta, the Confederate armies in the west never again poised a serious threat to the Union army.

Chester initially enlisted in Company B, 9th Battalion Cavalry, Georgia State Guards in August, 1863, but by June re-enlisted in the 5th Georgia Cavalry. His military records state that he was paroled at Hillsboro, N.C., May 3, 1865, after General Johnston surrendered to General Sherman (April 28, 1865).

Hickory Level, Carroll, Ga.,
December 15, 1863.

Dear Mother:

I think it is high time that I was writing home after a silence of nearly a month. I have not written sooner because for two weeks after Mr. Faw left for home I was at Mr. Ridleys where there is no regular mail and of course I found no other opportunity of sending a letter—when I arrived at this place I expected to go home soon and I therefore thought it unnecessary to write. When I arrived I found a letter from you and Lizzie, which although old was very welcome. I received later news from you through Mr. Faw, who said that Lizzie was getting better although by no means well.

When I reached this place which was on last Tuesday I found only three of my company here and I concluded not to apply for a furlough at present as there was considerable complaint in the Battalion because so many of our men had already gone home.

Capt. Rice came in yesterday and says he has orders not to give any furloughs except in urgent cases, but I think I will have no difficulty in getting one when the others come back which will not be long I think.

My horse is a good deal better though not well yet, I got him fat at Mr. Ridley's during the two weeks that I was there. I had a very pleasant time while I was there, and when I went to start I asked the old man what my bill was he told me that if I wanted to pay anything just to pay for the corn that my horse had eaten. I made a sort of rough calculation of the amount and told him what it was, and he said just to pay him five dollars and that would be sufficient, and it was all he would receive, and he told me whenever I came near to come and see them, which invitation I think I shall be very apt to expect /accept/ if I ever have an opportunity. I took considerable cold during the first part of my stay at Mr. Ridley's from which I am recovering since I have got back into camp.

Lieutenant Robertson tells us that Jouett is writing for Mr. Young and says he is the "greatest boy to write he ever saw." I am very glad he has got at it I expect it will be a great improvement to him.

As I said before Capt. Rice has arrived and with him strict orders he has instituted two drills a day and regular hours, which I am glad of, although it is very unacceptable to a good many of the Battalion. Under Capt. Loveless' regime there were no drills at all and roll call was abolished entirely.

Capt. Rice came with the expectation of assuming the command of the Battalion which was also Major Phillips understanding but on arriving he found that Capt. Reid of the Haralson company outranked him his commission being 10 days older. Capt. Reid has not been with us very long (he and his company came in at Bowdon) but he is pretty generally liked. I took dinner at his house once, before he came into the Battalion, when I was a scout in his county.

The cows and hogs are worse about this place than at any we have been to before and rocks are so scarce that they rob and plunder almost with impunity. To guard against the attacks of enemies of this kind, Mr. Faw and I went out and made us a trough and put it up high enough to be out of their reach. We performed our work so nicely that we have to go out and look and it every now and then. Just as I had finished writing the above I was called to, and told that my horse had lain down and got fastened so that he could not get up. I went out and sure enough I found not my horse indeed, but Mr. Faw's fastened down under our famous trough. I released him and with an air of great satisfaction he trotted off and I had to tramp off through the woods and get him and tie him again. I was very glad on my arrival here to find your nice present—the day I started was very cold and I tried at every house on the road to buy a pair of gloves and did not succeed, though at one house a woman told me she had an old pair which she would give me if they would do me any good, of course I accepted them and although they were somewhat moth eaten they were very warm and as they are very large for me they will do to go over the others and protect them.

Tell Pa I am much obliged to him for the money, I was not out but it will not be wasted on that account. Give my best love all after taking a portion for yourself and look for me at home before long.

Yours,

O.D. Chester

Marietta June 30/64

Dear Father:

I write this without knowing where to send it, but I hope you will get it and it is very important for you to come back if you can, for you left without letting Mr. Howell and others who calculated on your staying know of it, and they are very much troubled about it. Mr. Howell says he told you that his staying depended upon your movements. I thought that you had left word with him about your going. I recollect that we spoke of the necessity of it. If you would write to Mr. H. and give him your direction so that he could inform you at what time you would be needed you would take a great load off his mind. I could not tell him where to write to you as I did not know certainly where you were going.

I leave tomorrow for my regiment which is now about a half mile the other side of Dunwoody's. I was up there this morning but came back in order to go to Atlanta to find some money for Uncle Mat. I have heard nothing from my bridle and expect never to see it again. Capt. Walthour says I can draw one.

I still think Marietta is safe although it seems very doubtful for our lines are nearer now than they were before you left. The firing last night was so heavy that it woke up Uncle Mat who has never before heard a cannon. The firing was a great deal heavier last night than ever before, but we found out this morning that it amounted to nothing.

I have been very well since your departure. I saw Brother Charlie yesterday and he informed me that he saw you at a distance in Atlanta on Monday evening, so I suppose you had some difficulty in getting off. We also saw Ma in Griffin the same day & I was sorry to learn from him that Lizzie was quite sick.

Aunt P or Molly is not well satisfied as I expected. I heard her make some remark as this: "Just wait till Mi-tis gets settled."

Our house is occupied by surgeons & chaplains and the whole front yard with hospital tents, but on the whole I think it looks better than could be expected. Dr. Ward don't give much attention to it. When I see anything going wrong I speak to him about it he attends to it but unless I do he don't notice.

I expected to write less than I have done but I have filled three pages it is now bedtime and I must close. Much love to you & Jouett.

Your affectionate son,

Devant Chester

P.S. Uncle Mat says he almost wishes he had gone with (six) because the soldiers worry him to death almost. He sends love. Please excuse mistakes as I write in hurry no time to review. Do, write to Mr. Howell. My address A.D.C. Co. G 5th Gen Anderson's Brigade Wheeler's Cav.

O. Devant Chester

Dear Sis Nina I direct this letter to you because I don't know where Pa is and perhaps you do please send this to him as soon as possible. Yours truly,

O. Devant Chester

Camp near Brown's Farm
Fulton, Ga.
July 8, 1864.

Dear Mother,

I have at least found time to write after a pretty busy time. I joined my regiment the Friday after you left and was put on picket in front of our lines. During the night our army fell back and our division was left behind to cover the retreat on the Atlanta Road, so when I came in from picket instead of going to sleep as I wanted to, I had to go on with the regiment without getting of my horse. We went on without stopping until we got a little past Mr. McLeod's where we were dismounted and formed into line on the Railroad and one or two companys /*sic*/ sent forward as Skirmishers into McLeoud's field. We all sat down on the Railroad where there happened to be a cut about 6 or 8 ft. deep. We had been there but a short while before a shell whistled over our head and exploded just on the other side in Judge Eve's lot. It passed so close that there was a general rush to the side of the cut where we remained until the firing was over. We were just between out own and the enemies batteries which were situated, the former on Judge Eve's hill and the latter near Mr. McLeod's house. The firing was continued about an hour or more when our guns were removed and the enemy's soon ceased. Fortunately, none of the shells fell on the Railroad where our company /was/. Several exploded over us but the pieces fell on the side of the Railroad. Some would fall on one side of the road and bounce across. One struck so near the edge just above me that it rolled the dirt down on me. One of our guns came very near doing us a great deal of damage. It was charged with Canister shots and they fell as they passed over very near to us. One of them struck just above Potter's head. When we left that place we went on a little past Mr. Barber's. There we had no Railroad to protect us and we had to build breastworks of rail on the track. We succeeded in getting pretty good protection against musketry before our skirmishers got down as far as we were. Pretty soon I could see the Yankees in Mr. Barber's yard firing at our skirmishers who were in the field in front of us. We stayed here a long time, our skirmishers having climbed over our works and got with us behind them. The Yankees got up in the Barber's house and fired down on us, the ball came pretty close, but it was not near as scary as the shells. After a while we could see the Yankees advancing in several lines on our front. We were then commanded to move from our Position. I expected that when we came out from behind the rails they would cut us all up, but by the goodness of God we got off without the loss of a man. After we left that place we were not under fire anymore that day. We marched on down the Railroad to Smyrna where we turned to the left and marched several miles farther when we stopped and waited for our horses that had been led on by the fourth man. While waiting for the horses, I laid down and went to sleep. I dreamed of cannon firing all the time and once or twice started up hearing a canteen rattle and taking it for shell bursting. I never was so worn out in my life as I was that day. The sun poured down on my head as I laid behind the rails and drew the perspiration out in streams. On the march I wanted water so badly that I was glad to drink water out of the mud puddles on the side of the road. On the retreat to the river we saw a better time, had no fighting to do and were on our horses. The Yanks shelled us as we crossed the river on the Pontoon bridge but did no damage although they threw their shells close.

We are now on the south side of the river, although the infantry is all on the other. I am glad to find that this is a great deal better position than I thought, and I hope that with the help of the river we will not be flanked out of this position. I stopped a little while in Marietta as we passed through to see Aunt Polly who I have found quite well and very glad to see me. I stayed only a minute; I did not hear anything of Uncle Mat or Aunt Martha. I have been very well so far, and have such an appetite that I enjoy my rations of cold cornbread and bacon very much indeed.

There is a creek near this place where I go every day and bathe, which is quite a luxury. If I could get my clothes washed I would be very well satisfied. I bogged up to my knees on the retreat to Marietta going into a swamp of water. I stood the march down better than a good many, although I had been up most all the night before and had not taken off my cartridge box and haversack since the evening before. While I was in the deep cut during the shelling a man in the next company was wounded about 10 or 15 steps from me. He was like the ostrich—had stuck his head and body under a little bridge and got shot in the exposed part. I hope I shall never be fired on so much without being able to return it. It is very difficult for me to write sitting on the ground. Please excuse this scrawl. I am anxiously awaiting a letter from you. Give a great deal of love to all, including Aunt Matilda's family.

Your affecionate,
O.D.C.

Bivouac 5th Ga. Cav.
Near Chattahoochee River
July 14th, 1864.

Dear Lizzie:

I have not heard from you for some time and then it was through your father who said that you were sick when he last saw you but that he thought you would soon be well, and I hope before this reaches you, you will be so.

I have not received a letter from any of you since the move. I have been in the army now about two weeks and have seen all sorts of times. I saw a very hard time on the retreat from Kenesaw /*sic*/. Our division was the last of the army and the enemy pressed us very closely, and we had to stop several times and build breastworks and hold them till the Yanks drove us out of them. Since that time we have not had such hard times. When we fall back to this side of the river we were not so closely pressed although we were again in the rear, and we were not fired on except as we were crossing the river. At that place the Yankees got close enough behind us to plant a battery on a hill near the river with which they shelled the pontoons /bridges/ as we crossed over but without doing any damage except scaring our horses (and some of the men too) although they threw their shells very close. I was on picket at the place where crossed and I could see the affects on the trees and ground. One tree about a foot through was cut almost down, and the ground was covered with limbs torn from trees. Our regiment is stationed near the river about two or three miles above the rail road bridge and we can hear the Yankee engines on the other side of the river.

The life here is very monotonous. When I am in camp (which is about every other day) when I get up the first thing I do is to get my haversack and take out a pone of corn bread, split it open and take a piece of bacon and hold it over the fire by means of a stick until the grease runs out of it, then let it drip on the bread, by the time the meat gets done, the bread is pretty well greased over, I then put the bread on a stick and hold it over the blaze until it gets a little brown, my breakfast is then cooked. Dinner & supper are the same, except when I am marching, when I have to eat the bacon raw, and the bread cold. It is astonishing to me how well I like the fare, I am always hungry and eat all I draw with the greatest relish.

We have been expecting to draw vegetables for some time but have not done so yet. Willie Baker came up to see us from Atlanta last week and his arm is not improving very fast.

I am very well pleased with the company I joined. Have you heard from Marietta since it has been occupied by the Yankees? I have heard very little. It is said that the Institute building has been burnt, and one of the Yankees told me that their suttlers keep their stores there.

I would like very much to hear from Aunt Martha and Uncle Mat and also from Aunt Polly. I saw Aunt Polly the day the Yankees took possession of the place. She was still at the old place but I expect she has gone up to Aunt Martha's before this. Aunt Martha told her to come up and stay in the old kitchen.

There is a rain coming up and I must close and look at my things. Tomorrow, if I am not on duty I expect to write Sis Mary, who I suppose is till with you.

Yours very affectionately,
Devant Chester

Chester also wrote a letter to Lizzie on the 14th. It is similar to the letter he wrote his sister. In it he also describes the shelling by Yankee troops.

Near Chattachoochee
Fulton Co.
July 15th, 1864.

Dear Sister -
——Pickets don't fire at each other now. We go down to the edge of the river on our side and the Yankees come down on their side and talk to each other. The men on picket opposite are from Ohio, and seem to be very tired of the war. They say that their term of enlistment will be out in three months and most of them say that when it is out they are going home. Gen. Johns/t/on has issued an order that there shall be no more communication between with them, and I think it is well that he has done so because they were

getting too intimate. Some men don't know what should be concealed. The Yankees are very much in want of tobacco, and our Government gives it to us, and we used to trade tobacco with them for knives and canteens. There is a rock near the middle of the river to which they would swim and trade. After a while they got so well acquainted that some of our men would swim clear across and land among the Yankees. The Yankees were not so bold for a long time, but a few days ago they got to coming across also. That has been broken up now and if any trading is carried on, it is done contrary to orders. —— I took some tobacco down with me the other day but I found out when I got there communication had been stopped. As I was sitting on the banks, one of the Yankees on the other side called to me to know if I had any tobacco. I told him I had. He said that he had a good knife to trade me for it. I told him that trading was prohibited. He said "Your officers won't see you, come over, I want a chew of tobacco very bad." I asked some of them who they were going to vote for President. One of them said "Old Abe" but most of them said they were for McLellan.

We have a fine rain last night that was much needed. I had my oil cloth pitched for a tent but it leaks very badly. I got rather wet but the rain was very hard and lasted only a short time, and I got dry and went back to bed and slept very well.

One of the Yankee Lieutenants promised to mail some letters for one of our officers and I wrote to Aunt Martha expecting to send it at the same time but Gen. Johns/t/on stopped the proceeding so I did not send it. There is a force of Yankees on this side of the river and have been there for some time. Why Gen. Johns/t/on don't drive them back I don't know, he must have some object in view.

Write to me soon.

Yours truly,

O.D. Chester

Wesley Chapel,
Dekalb County, Ga.
 In Bivouic /sic/
July 26, 1864.

Dear Father:

I had not got ready to write to you when your very welcome letter was handed me. It was the first time I heard from you directly since I saw you. I received a letter from sister Mary but she merely told me that you were in Fort Valley and supposed that I had heard from you. I would like to write oftener than I do but I have very little time to write. I am most of the time in the saddle, more than ever since we crossed the Chattahoochee. We have just returned from Conyers, near Convington where we went after the raiding party that has been destroying the Georgia Railroad. After riding as far as Conyers we were sent back, it being supposed that our force was larger than necessary. I was very, sorry indeed that we were turned back. I think I would like pursuing a party of raiders better than any service I have been engaged in although it is very hard on both horses and men. I have started at daybreak or sooner and ridden till after midnight without stopping long enough to unsaddle and then lying down with all my things on and without unrolling my blanket or un-saddling my horse and slept with my gun for a pillow. We have been separated from our wagons for some time and consequently have been very much in need of food. There are so many of us that the Citizens cannot supply us all, though they do a great deal. Our wagons came up today and we got a supply of hard tack and bacon so for the time we are doing finely. I had a fine dinner today. Procter and I went out and found a very nice house and plantation that had been hurridly /sic/ abandoned by the owners. The rascally heart of the soldiery had been there and torn things to pieces. It is wonderful to see how far they carry the work of destruction. They even took down the clock and broke it all to pieces. They tore down the bedsteads and broke open the bee hives which they partially robbed, leaving the honey scattered over the grounds. We got as much as we wanted to eat but had no way of carrying any of it away. We then went to the garden where we got a fine bagful of Irish potatoes and plenty of wheat for our horses which we brought off. When we got to camp we very unexpectedly drew a little flour. I then went to a house and begged a woman out of a little salt. We then borrowed a spider and baking pan and went to cooking. Procter made the bread and I cooked the potatoes and meat and when the potatoes were done I added water and boiled my hard tack in the liquor. When it was all done we invited a few friends and had a fine time. I enjoy starving and hard riding a great deal better than I expected. Our Company (G) has been separated from the regiment and temporaryly /sic/ connected with the 8th Confederate who are not always engaged when the rest of us are but are kept in the rear ready to advance at any moment. If it were not so late I would give you a long account of our dash into Decatur. We were held back until the Yankees commenced to run when we charged after them at a break neck gallop, capturing some prisoners and considerable plunder. I myself made no captures except in the eating line. I went into a little shop where some officers had been cooking and pounced upon a pot of beef that was just done and very nice. I had had nothing for some time. I tried some coffee I found on the table but it was too much shaken up.

Give my love to Ma and Joeutt.

O.D. Chester

I am very well and enjoying myself, finely. Joe Roberts was wounded slightly the other day, the only man in the Company that has been hurt.

O.D.C

P.S. Do write as often as you can and direct— Company G 5th. Ga. Reg.

Anderson's Brigade

Wheeler's Corps

Army of Tenn.

Oxford, Ga.

August 9, 1864.

Dera Janett -

————We advanced awhile together and then our company led by Capt. Walthorn went across a field in order to charge some that were on a hill. We found such a bog that had to turn back. In going back we were fired into by the Yankees, some of whom had come down to cut us off. They had a splendid chance at us as we passed them in an open field. The rascals slipped by us and went toward Covington. We got back to where we left the Brigade a little after dark and found that it had gone after the other raid, the one that passed through Newnan. I wish very much I could have been with them. They captured a great many prisoners and horses. Proctor made more captures than any man in the company. He got two horses, 8 saddles, 4 pair of sadddle bags, 2 or 3 good bridles, 2 halters, some coffee, tobacco, salt, etc. He gave me a pair of saddle bags. ————————I was separated from the regiment at Newnan. I stayed with Mr. Caldwell the Methodist Minister. He passed me just as I was asking if there were any Refugees from Marietta, he stopped and inquired my name, gave me a pressing invitation to go home with him, which I did.

    O.D. Chester

Glade Spring/s/, Va.

Oct. 5, 1864.

Dear Mother,

    I expect that you have received a short note that I wrote a few days ago. I wrote them in a great hurry and with few conveniences for writing. We started on this raid expecting it to last only a week or at least that was my expectation and were ordered to carry as little with us as possible, in fact to take no clothes except those we had on and no blanket except what was under our saddles. Some obeyed this order to the letter, but I did not like the idea of going off without my clothes and as I had a small part of my saddle bags that were likely to go unnoticed in the inspection I put all my clothes in them except one shirt which with my blanket I left with the wagon at Convigton. I have congratulated myself ever since that I did so for although I didn't have time to clean clothes that I had served me for one change which was a great deal better than to be obliged to go for two months with the same clothes.

    Gen. Wheeler with the principal part of his command got out of Tenn. some time before we did. Our Brigade together with that of Gen. Williams have cut off from him at Emory river the principal part of the army crossed in evening and we were to follow on the next morning but the river rose so much during the night that it was unfordable by morning and one had to travel up it for two days before we found a crossing place. We then set out and made the rest of the raid on our own hook and we came out rather more successfully than Wheeler himself for the Yankees only got after us once, and then although we had to fight one whole day with them we lost only one man killed and a few wounded. Among the latter was Proctor Lawrence who received a slight wound in the forehead of which he has entirely recovered. It was wonderful that he was hurt no worse.

It was evidently providential that we were cut off since we were obliged to come out through Virginia I got here in time to anticipate the Yankee raid on the salt works on account of which you have seen I suppose. I am so anxious to hear from home and I am afraid it will be some time before I shall be able to hear, however I would be glad if you would write and run the risk of my getting it.

Tell me how Lizzie is and how Jonettt's eyes are, where Sis, Mary is and what is your own and the general opinion of "Secesh" now. You don't know how badly I want to see you all. I don't know whether we will go back to Georgia or not but suppose we will. The men generally are anxious to get back, as for myself, if I could hear from home regularly I would rather be here I believe.

The people of Middle Run were very glad to see us and gave us a warm reception. I was very much pleased with Tenn. I would like to write more but have no paper. Ask sister Mary to send me cousin Millie's direction. Give much love to all.

Your very loving son,

O.D. Chester

Lizzie died on August 24.

Washington, Ga.
October 27, 1864.
Dear Sister:
At Greenville, S.C. Proctor had his horse stolen, traced thief to Augusta. Heard of death of 2 cousins since he last saw Marietta, 4 months ago. Hardly slept last night but when he did he dreamed of Marietta and saw all the Yankees had done there.

We both, when we left the regiment were ragged and dirty. Proctor went to the Hospital and Relief Association at Augusta and got a coat and shirt his being in rags. Before we got to Augusta, we passed through a little town called Williamston, I proposed to Proctor that he had four hats that he brought from Shelbyville, he should take them to a store and exchange them for a pair of boots which he needed very much, he told me to take them and see what I could do with them and I succeeded in getting two pair of boots for three hats and so we both got a pair and altogether our appearance is so much improved that we feel quite stylish.

Your brother,
O.D. Chester

Bivouac 5th Ga. Cav.
near Columbia, S.C.
Feb. 18, 1865
Dear Janett,
I received a letter from sister Mary a day or two ago and one from sister a short time before both of which I derived a great deal of pleasure being the first news I had had from them since I left. You are still in bed I suppose but I hope you will soon be up again. We have just evacuated Columbia after holding it only two days. It does seem as if there is nothing in the Confederacy except Wheeler's cavalry. I expected that when we got to Columbia we would find a large infantry force there, at least enough to hold the Yankees back a while but there turned out to be only a Brigade or two and they fell back into the city and burned the bridge the very night we got

up to them. The next morning the Yankees brought a battery up so near that they would throw shells right into the heart of town. The Governor of South Carolina had all the stores closed and a provost guard stationed at the door of each to prevent the soldiers from prowling, consequently when the Yankees got possession of the place they got enough of everything to last till they got into Richmond. I am speaking rather extravagantly /*sic*/ but they did get a great deal. Some of the Tenneseans /*sic*/ and Texans broke some stores and helped themselves—one of them gave me the pencil I am writing with. We had a splendid time chasing Kilpatrick the other day at Aiken.

Wheeler formed his men somewhat in the shape of a V triangle, the angle of which was bisected by the railroad and a road running parallel with it, on which the Yankees were advancing and placed a small force at the opening of the V with orders to fight them a little while and I think to stampede and draw them in and they charged them on both flanks. Consequently the Yankees got started back before we got among them but we saw them about 5 miles firing into their column all the while. We had a right sharp fight with them before they understood that we were whipping them and in it I got struck for the first time with a minnie ball. It struck a tree first and glanced and hit me on the leg just above the knee. It bruised me a little and caused a slight swelling but did not hurt me much. Henry Russell of our company was shot in the head about the same time but injured so little that he was ready for duty the next day. I could not learn anything about cousin Bessie in Columbia, not being able to find anyone that knew her. My love to all.

Yours affectionately,

O.D. Chester

I write this without knowing when I will have an opportunity of sending it.

This was Chester's last letter. His company surrendered along with Johnston's forces at Greensboro, N.C. on May 3.

Johnny Reb am I

I'm a Confederate as if I fired the missile on Sumter
that fateful day.
With gray on my back and rags on my feet, I march on,
My destiny.
My musket and I, my haversack, my powder,
Pride in my Johnny Reb heart.
First the glory of war, then the heartbreak of
a thousand comrades slain,
My land is ruined, pillaged and plundered,
I wipe the tear from my eye,
The ranks are all thin, there's not much gray to cover the soldier's
back,
The enemy swells, he grows proud and he's strong...
I stop to catch my breath.
Johnny Reb am I, Johnny Reb I pray,
Lay down your musket and walk away.

Bibliography

Anderson, Robert H., letter to Gen. Braxton Bragg. *Benjamin Remington Armstrong & Alexander Armstrong papers*. Georgia Historical Society, Savannah.

Barnard, J.D. *Georgia Confederate Pension*. Georgia Department of Archives and History, Atlanta.

Bird, James. *Biographical Sketch of James Bird*. Georgia Department of Archives and His-tory, Atlanta.

Boatner, Mark M. III. *The Civil War Dictionary*. New York: David McKay Companies, Inc., 1980.

Burge, Dolly Sumner Lunt. *A Woman's War Time Journal*. Atlanta, Georgia: Cherokee Pub-lishing Co., 1944.

Cay, Raymond. *Capture Remount Detachment of the Liberty Independent Troop*. Georgia Department of Archives and History, Atlanta.

Cay, Raymond. *Confederate Pension File*. Georgia Department of Archives and History, Atlanta.

Chester, Orlando Devant. *Letters of O. Devant Chester*. Kennesaw Mountain National Battle-field Park, Kennesaw.

Chester, Orlando Devant. *Confederate Pension File*. Georgia Department of Archives and History, Atlanta.

Current, Richard Nelson. *Lincoln's Loyalists: Union Soldiers from the Confederacy*. New York: Oxford University Press, 1992.

Current, Richard N., ed. *Encyclopedia of the Confederacy*. New

York: Simon & Schuster. n.d.

Davis, Burke. *Sherman's March*. New York: Random House, 1980.

DeLoach, Zachariah Taylor. *Reminiscences and Biographical sketch of Z.T. DeLoach*. Georgia Department of Archives and History, Atlanta.

Donald, David, ed., *Why The North Won The Civil War*. Baton Rouge: LSU Press, 1962.

Dorsey, B.W. *A War Story or My Experiences in a Yankee Prison*. Georgia Department of Archives and History, Atlanta.

Dyer, John P. *Fightin' Joe Wheeler*. Baton Rouge: LSU Press, 1941.

Edenfield, H.G. *Letters of H.G. Edenfield*. Georgia Department of Archives and History, Atlanta.

Evans, Clement A., ed. *Confederate Military History, Extended Edition* 1889. Reprint. Wilmington, North Carolina: Broadfoot Publishing Co., 1987.

Fifth Georgia Regiment Cavalry (Lamar Rangers). *Muster and Payroll July 11, 1862*. Georgia Historical Society, Savannah.

Hansen, Harry. *The Civil War: A History*. New York: Penguin Books, 1961.

Henderson, William Michael. *Biographical and Military Sketch of W.M. Henderson*. Geor-gia Department of Archives and History, Atlanta.

Hesseltine, William B. *Civil War Prisons: A Study in War Psychology*. Ohio State University: Ohio State Press, 1930.

Houston, Thomas Wayman. *Sketch of Thomas Wayman Houston from the Ludawici News June 8, 1967*. Georgia Department of Archives and History, Atlanta.

Jones, John B. *A Rebel War Clerk's Diary*. Baton Rouge: LSU Press, 1993.

Jones, Katherine M., ed. *Heroines of Dixie: Winter of Desparation*. St. Simmons Island, Georgia: Mockingbird Books, Inc., 1990.

Johnson, Robert U., and Clarence C. Buel, eds. *Battles and Leaders of the Civil War*. 4 vols. 1887. Reprint. Secaucus, New Jersey: Castle, n.d.

Lambright, J.T. *History of the Independent Troop During Civil War, 1862-65*. Georgia Historical Society, Savannah.

Lee, James Robert. *Biographical Sketch of R.J. Lee*. Georgia Department of Archives and History, Atlanta.

Livermore, Thomas L. *Numbers and Losses in the Civil War in America*. Cambridge: The University Press, 1901.

Long, E.B. *The Civil War Day By Day: An Almanac 1861-1865*. Garden City, New York: Doubleday, 1971.

McCarley, J. Britt. *The Atlanta Campaign: A Civil War Driving Tour of Atlanta Area Battle-fields*. Atlanta, Georgia: Cherokee Publishing Co., 1984.

McPherson, James M. *What They Fought For 1861-1865*. New York: Doubleday, 1994.

Mitchell, Patricia B. *Yanks, Rebels, Rats, & Rations: Scratching For Food in Civil War Prison Camps*. Chatham, Virginia: Patricia B. Mitchell, 1993.

Southern Historical Society Papers. 52 vols. 1876-1959. Reprint. Millwood, New York: Kraus Reprint Co., 1977.

Tancig, W.J. *Confederate Military Land Units*. Cranbury, New Jersey: Thomas Yoseloff Publisher, 1967.

Thomas, Emory M. *The Confederacy as a Revolutionary Experience*, Columbia, South Carolina: University of South Carolina Press, 1991.

Thorpe, Samuel J. Nar*rative from the Atlanta Journal,* March 16, 1901.

U.S. War Department. *The War of the Rebellion: A Compilation of the Union and Confeder-ate Armies*. 70 vols. in 128 parts. 1880-1901. Reprint. Harrisburg, Pennsylvania: His-torical Times, 1985.

Wagner, Bernard C, *Letters of Bernard C. Wagner*. Georgia Department of Archives and History, Atlanta.

Waring, Joseph Fredick. *The Joseph Fredrick Waring Papers: The Jeff Davis Legion*. Geor-gia Historical Society, Savannah.

Wiley, Irvin Bell. *The Life of Johnny Reb: The Common Soldier of the Confederacy*. Baton Rouge: LSU Press, 1943.

Civil War Re-enactment

David and Joan Hagan

Re-enacting the Civil War battles in authentic costumes has become a growing hobby among the general population today. Popular with novice and historian alike, the human drama of the Civil War is brought alive through study, folk skills and stories, and re-living events of a hundred and thirty years ago. Photographers David and Joan Hagan portray this drama through their poignant pictures taken during re-enacted battles. With a little imagination you become part of the action, hear the gunfire and shouting, and smell the smoke through their brilliant close-up photography. Authentic clothing, implements, food and environment are strictly reproduced. These pictures transport you to another time and place where daily life was disrupted and each person struggled with life-threatening conditions.
Size: 8 1/2" x 11 ■ over 290 color photographs ■ 112 pp.
ISBN: 0-88740-949-0 ■ soft cover ■ $19.95

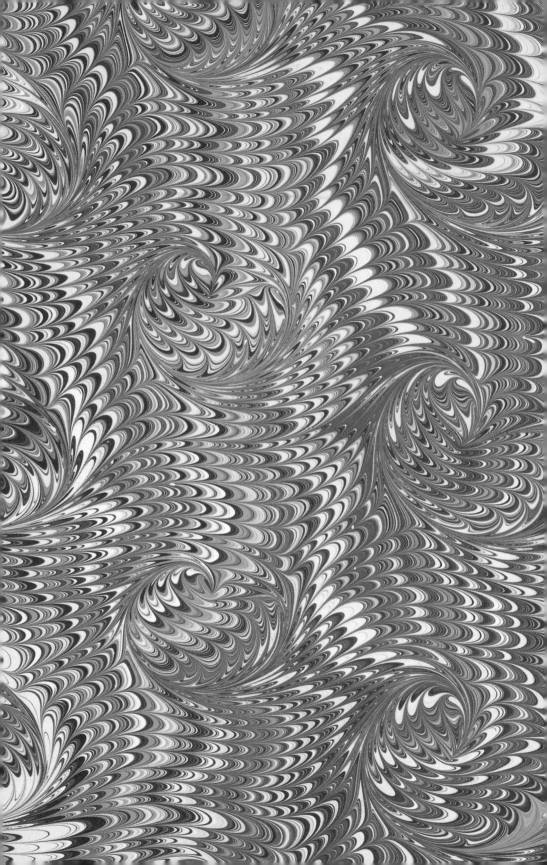